Believe It Or Not?

FOLKLORE,
WITCHCRAFT AND
MAGICAL THINKING
FROM THE
NORTH YORK MOORS,
COAST AND CLEVELAND

Esk Valley News

First published by Esk Valley News, 2024

© 2024 Copyright of texts and photographs remains with their authors

All rights reserved. No part of this publication may be reproduced, stored in a retrieval system or transmitted in any form or by any means, electronic, mechanical, photocopying, recording or otherwise, without the prior written permission of the copyright owners.

A Catalogue in Publication record for this book is available from the British Library

ISBN: 978-1-7385578-0-6

Printed and bound in the UK by Mixam (www.mixam.co.uk)
This book is produced using paper stocks from sustainable sources and superior-quality vegetable-based inks.

Esk Valley News
The Old Parsonage
Glaisdale, Whitby YO21 2PL

Many of the articles in this book were first published in *Esk Valley News Quarterly*, a not-for-profit community engagement magazine for the North York Moors, Coast and Cleveland. For more information see: www.eskvalleynews.co.uk

Contents

7   Foreword

WITCHES, MAGIC & FOLK HEALING

11   The Prolonged Persecution of North York Moors 'Witches'
26   Local Witches and Their Attributes According to the Calvert Manuscript
28   Moorland Witch Places
29   The 'Witch' from Marske
30   Witch's Broom
31   The Curious Case of the Region's 'Witch Posts'
34   Protective Markings – X Marks the Spot!
35   Concealed Objects Hidden Across Homes
37   A Concealed Spoon at Harome Hall – But Why?
40   Folk Healing and Magical Thinking
42   Herbal Wisdom of the Past: Moorland Dew

FAIRIES, CREATURES, GHOSTS & LEGENDS

47   Hobs of the North York Moors
48   Hobs, Goblins, Boggles and Sprites
52   The Hob Song
53   The Hobman of Upleatham
56   Handale Priory
57   The Tale of the Handale Wyrm
61   The Man from Upsall / A Guisborough Legend
62   The Hermit of Falling Foss / Nunnington Church Tomb
63   The Story of the Nunnington Dragon
66   Fairy Rings
72   Antiquities of Goathland
75   The Gytrash of Goathland
83   The Mysterious Beast of the Moors

85	Bell and Wade: A Tale of Two Giants
86	Creatures Beneath the Waves
88	They Have a Legend Here That When a Ship is Lost Bells are Heard out at Sea…
92	The Hand of Glory
93	Gibbets and Gallows
96	Moor Ghosts
101	The Lockwood Beck Ghost Pack
103	Following the Threads of Kitty and her Sark

BELIEFS, RITUALS & TRADITIONS

107	The Lyke Wake Walk … Inspired by a Song
111	The Lyke Wake Dirge
112	Corn Dollies
113	Westerdale's Corn Spirits & Corn Dollies
117	Here We Come A Wassailing
123	Whitby's Ceremony of the Penny Hedge
127	The Foretelling of Thunder
128	Here We Go Round… the Kissing Ring
129	How to Find Your Valentine
131	Sword Dancing
132	Longsword Dancing in the Esk Valley and East Cleveland
134	The Goathland Plough Stots
137	Plough Monday: An Old Yorkshire Tradition
138	Cloggers in Arncliffe
140	Clog Dancing
142	A Yacre of Land – a Folk Song
143	Ralph Vaughan Williams' Visit to Westerdale
145	The Krampus Run Has Come to Whitby

Foreword

The beliefs, traditions and stories that you'll encounter in this book speak of the profound connection which the people of this region have had with the land, their work and daily lives, and with each other. These things form the basis of a common culture wherever you happen to be in the world, but I always find that those beliefs and practices which push at the boundaries of normality are usually the most interesting. This is why an anthology such as this one – with all its wyrms, witches, ghosts and boggarts – is especially captivating for me and I hope will hold a world of wonder for you too.

My own particular fascination is with witchcraft beliefs, shown here through an array of objects, including crystal balls, 'spell tokens', so-called 'witch posts', and many other items which must have been equally enthralling within their own times as in ours. One practice included that I have long been captivated by is that of making a 'witch bottle'. Such objects help create a tangible link with the people of the past. These bottles were originally created inside an anthropomorphic bottle and contained an individual's urine, hair, nail parings and bent pins. It's thought these items acted together as a lure because they contained the essence of the victim. However, they were also a trap since they were buried upside down, containing pins and nails which had been deliberately 'killed' by being bent before going into the bottle.

Such objects have so much to teach us about the beliefs that people held at the time, the power sought by individuals to influence their own fates, and the way people perceived the nature of the objects around them. By taking a look at just one slightly unusual story or practice, we can uncover such a lot about their lives…

…And inside this book there are so many unusual beliefs and practices to wonder at. The fear people had of the supernatural was, by today's standards, all pervasive. There were apotropaic (protective) marks for keeping evil at bay, old shoes for use as decoys, dead cats for warding off lesser spells, and herbal charms and written incantations for almost anything else.

For the majority of people in pre-modern societies, there was a perception that supernatural forces existed all around us and that it was only positive action that could keep us safe. Letting one's guard down was believed to result in illness, misfortune, bewitchment and, ultimately, even death.

This book explores stories from a time that can often feel remote and inaccessible to us. For centuries, if someone suspected they were under the influence of some maleficent spell then the assistance of the 'cunning folk' was often sought to help with any perceived bewitchment. These were the local 'white' witches (who were often in reality a bit 'grey'). They would most usually barter or trade for their services and might perform love spells for individuals, detect thieves, diagnose illnesses and produce charms. They were even believed to detect maleficium (bad magic) and identify local 'bad' witches.

Can you imagine what life would be like now, if we held the same witchcraft beliefs as were held in the past? Life would certainly be a lot stranger and perhaps hold more to concern and worry us.

This collection seeks to capture something of this history of folk life, bringing many lesser-known British beliefs into the spotlight, with a particular focus on the special regions of the North York Moors and Ryedale. I hope that you will take away a sense of wonder that the landscape was (and perhaps still is) the location of wyrms, witches, ghosts, boggarts and some very curious stories and places.

BRIAN HOGGARD

Brian Hoggard is the author of *Magical House Protection* and www.apotropaios.co.uk.

1

WITCHES, MAGIC & FOLK HEALING

The Prolonged Persecution of North York Moors 'Witches'

'If rumour be true, some of the English rural districts, especially Yorkshire, are overrun with fraudulent astrologers and fortune-tellers.' [1] Madame Balavatsky

The old name for the North York Moors is 'Blackamoor'. Martyn Hudson's moving evocation of this moorland, *On Blackamoor*,[2] brings to mind its darker features: windswept peaty surfaces, the browned heather and charcoaled twisted roots from autumn burnings, a westerly roll of menacing storm clouds and the silent dim light of a blanket fog. At sundown, the great black hulk of the moor rises up and in its shadows lurk ghosts of long-abandoned cottages, hobs (fairies) and fearsome witches.

At the heart of this landscape Ryedale Folk Museum[3] at Hutton-le-Hole boasts an impressive collection on the moor's folklore and social history. Museum curator Bert Frank (1919–1996) was fascinated in local 'witch-lore'; his notebooks held in the Museum record the memories of older inhabitants and the contents of a manuscript ('The Calvert Manuscript'). George Calvert is thought to have written the manuscript when he was living on the edge of the moors at Kirkbymoorside in 1823.

In Calvert's time, 'every village had its witch', and the 'witches' in the region were 'great in number'. Calvert describes them as 'old women… called witch-haggs or witch wives… mostly single, or widows with no family, often ugly, the hardships they were compelled to undergo in order to live having contributed to this'. Their homes were called 'hovels'.[4] The local vicar of Danby from 1847 to 1898, Reverend J.C. Atkinson, paints a similar picture in a recollection from his first arrival in the village: 'the whole atmosphere of the folklore firmament in this district was so surcharged with the being and the works of the witch, that one seemed able to trace her presence and her activity in almost every nook and corner of the neighbourhood.'[5]

Closer to our times, Percy Shaw Jeffrey in 1923 relates a story showing the entrenchment of local 'witch-lore' beliefs of people living in his day. His friend, Dr Thomas English (1865–1937), was treating a patient suffering from influenza who was convinced that his affliction was due to a woman at Whitby market who had given him the 'evil eye'. The unfortunate man thought she had bewitched him so had asked Dr English for a 'Wise Man's' remedy to counteract her magic. Dr English, seeing that his patient truly believed he was under a spell, proceeded to dispense an 'old remedy' to deal with such things but warned the patient not to tell anyone else or the remedy wouldn't work. In the bottle prescribed of course the doctor mixed the usual remedy for influenza and the man soon recovered.[6]

Another example is the unfortunate man from Fylingthorpe who believed he himself had the 'evil eye' and was so afraid he would harm someone that he walked everywhere with his head bent and eyes fixed to the ground.[7]

Fear of witches fed into the everyday life of fishermen in nearby Staithes. It was customary for them to blame a run of bad luck on a witch and to perform a ritual to flush her out: at midnight they would kill a pigeon, take out its heart, stick the heart full of pins and burn it. Whoever came to the door after the bird had turned to ashes would be deemed the witch responsible for their misfortune, drawn by the spell the fishermen had cast. But rather than punish the witch they would offer a present. And when their luck changed for the better they knew the witch was satisfied with their gift.[8]

NAMED 'WITCHES' OF BLACKAMOOR

By the time Calvert and Atkinson were collecting witch stories in the nineteenth century it was an offence in England to claim that any human being had magical powers or was guilty of practising witchcraft. This was the directive of the 1735 Witchcraft Act, replacing previous witchcraft legislation criminalising witches. The newly enlightened state professed to be rooting out 'ignorance, superstition, criminality and insurrection'.[9] However, this cultural shift apparently had little impact on the remote moorland communities of North Yorkshire. Local people willingly gave to collectors the names and localities of real inhabitants they believed to have been, or were still, 'witches' using magical powers.

Named local 'witches' recorded in George Calvert's Manuscript and by Canon Atkinson include:

- Nancy Nares of Pickering
- Hester Mudd of Rosedale

Emma Todd's crystal ball at Ryedale Folk Museum.

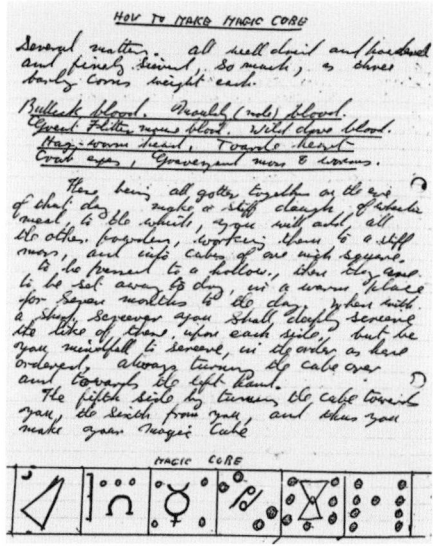

Magic cube markings from the Calvert Manuscript, as recorded in Bertram Frank's notebooks.

- Dina Suggest of Levisham
- Sally Craggs of Allerston
- Emma Todd of Ebberston
- Nan Scaife of Spaunton Moor near Hutton-le-Hole, who was said to have remarkable powers of foretelling events. Calvert collected a recipe she allegedly used to make magic cubes which included the ground-up powder of bone from the skull of a gibbeted man, the powder of which was kept in a glass vial for seven years. Added to this was bullock blood, mouldy (mole) blood, great flitter mouse (bat) blood, wild dove blood, hag-worm head, toad heart, crab eyes, graveyard moss and worms. The mixture was pressed into cube shapes, left to dry over seven months and the six sides of each cube were then inscribed.
- Sabina Moss of Cropton, who became known as 'Old Mother Migg' after she was tossed into a 'slag of migg' (manure). The smell was said to discourage people from visiting her 'hovel' thereafter.
- Peggy Dvell (or 'Devell') of Hutton-le-Hole who, with 'Old Susan', was said to travel to Malton to tell people's fortunes.

Copy of page of Peggy Dvell's magic book at Ryedale Folk Museum.

THE PAST DEMONISATION OF WITCHES

Keith Thomas's influential book *Religion and the Decline of Magic*[10] traces the roots of witch persecution in England to persistent attempts by Church reformers and other organs of state to stamp out pre-Christian Pagan magical beliefs.

Between 500 and 1,000 people are estimated to have died in England during the persecution, 90 per cent of whom were women.[11] Many were forced to betray others under torture. Those condemned to die by hanging or burning included 'witches' using 'black magic' for evil purposes – but also those offering magical solutions to everyday problems suffered by others (misfortune, ill health, unrequited love, economic difficulties, theft, etc), the so-called 'white witches'. Their proffered solutions from outside the auspices of the Church were seen to threaten the Church's monopoly of the truth, encouraging faithful parishioners to believe in magical powers of 'witchcraft' to solve life's woes. It became imperative for the Church and other organs of state to distinguish between the miracles from God associated with the Church and the magical powers of 'witches', and so it was deemed, and popularly accepted, that 'witches' were in league with the Devil. The outcome was the passing of the Witchcraft Act in 1541, the first Act in England to make witchcraft a crime punishable by death. Subsequent Acts refined the legislation. Following the state decrees came witch hunts and trials, at their most intense during the seventeenth century.[12]

Shakespeare's play *Macbeth* (1606) is believed to have been written to please King James I, who was fully in favour of the death penalty for witches.[13] Its depiction of the three 'weird sisters' has a devilish flavour: they lurk in the shadows with potions of 'eye of newt and toe of frog', speak in rhyme and demonstrate a power to summon supernatural powers to cause mischief and evil. These and other fearsome images of witches became part of the collective imagination and continue to inform witch stereotypes today.

Remote Blackamoor was spared the worst trauma of the organised witch-hunts and there were no local burnings of 'witches', although one case of 'witch' murder is recorded, of Meg Collett drowned in 1719 in Iburndale Beck near Sleights, as part of a local ducking.[14] Witchcraft practices and beliefs on the moors of North Yorkshire carried on relatively undisturbed, away from the gaze of the authorities. This might have been a peaceful continuation of tradition, but a fear of local witches, set in motion by demonic associations introduced by the Church, continued to feed the collective imagination. In the harsh living environment of the moors there were plentiful opportunities for pointing a finger of blame – for ill health, poverty, death of a child, theft, bad luck, a cow's loss of milk, even the poor weather – on women living alone who were believed to be practising 'black magic' and causing mischief.

CONTINUING A MAGICAL TRADITION

'The witches were enmeshed in the same landscape as the Norse goddesses and the Celtic spirits of the becks and rivers. Like the rock strata these mythologies were sedimentary, each successive layer laid down upon another in erratic ways . . . .'[15]

The collected witch stories of Blackamoor suggest that witchcraft and magical beliefs continued to be a way of life for people living on the moors well into

Macbeth consults the three witches. Engraving by W. Byrne, 1773.

the nineteenth century, and included 'white witches' who provided inhabitants with services of prophecy, treatment for illness and other remedies.

Their knowledge, skills and magical practices can be traced to the valued services of 'healers', 'herbalists' and 'wise men and women' of earlier Anglo-Saxon communities. *Bald's Leechbook*, written in the mid-ninth to early tenth century, now held at the British Library in London, gives an insight into early medieval healing remedies. These range from remarkably progressive remedies to unusual mixes of prayers, charms (magic spells), remnants of botanical studies and medical practices from antiquity, folklore and superstition. An example of the progressive type is a recipe for a nettle-based ointment for muscular pain that is similar to ointments available today. The more unusual include a treatment for swollen eyes (put the cut-off eyes from a live crab against the neck of the patient after returning the blinded crab to the water), and one for 'fiend sick', or demonic possession (drink an infusion of herbs out of a church bell).[16]

The old remedies offered by the nineteenth-century witches of Blackamoor were no doubt flavoured with traditions of Norse and other settlers, but their roots lay in a healing tradition passed down from pre-Christian Anglo-Saxon communities.

LEGENDS AND FEAR OF WITCHES

Over time, legends and folklore have grown up around the local people accused of witchcraft, their stories embellished over generations.

Nanny Pierson is a famous name associated with witchcraft in the village of Goathland. She could have been a woman named Ann Pierson who appears in the local burial register in 1849. In local witch stories Nanny Pierson is portrayed as fearsome and manipulative. She was blamed for many misfortunes, including the crippling of an unborn child.

The story of Nan Hardwick, a famous 'witch' of Danby folklore, is recorded by Canon Atkinson. She could have been the daughter of Matthew Hardwick, baptised in 12 May 1765. In the story she is an isolated woman picked on by local youth who, though fearing her, derived fun from chasing her. Canon Atkinson records one such Nan-chase:

'Down this cause it was the witch's custom, when she was thus chivied, to run at headlong speed, and as she wore clogs… the clatter of her footsteps could be heard long before she arrived near the foot of the slope'. One lad, Thomas Prudom, standing by the running water at Ainthorpe and blocking her path, was shocked to find she had disappeared and yet had the feeling of something rushing between his legs, enough to knock him over, the 'thing' uttering 'a weird sort of chuckling laugh'.[17] The idea was the traditional one of the witch having turned into a hare. A typical example of these stories, shared with Scandinavian repertoires, is that of a witch-hare stealing milk from cows in their pasture. Usually the hare can only be destroyed when shot by a silver bullet. If it is injured, accusers find the 'witch' sheltering in her hovel in human form suffering from a wound similar to the wound inflicted on the animal.

A legend about nearby Howe Wood, Kildale, associating the Devil with witches is referred to in this nineteenth-century rhyme: 'The Devil with his imps, His pleasure in the Kildale woods, There summer days did take…'. The traditional story finds Yeoman Stephen Howe boasting that if he caught the Devil with his imps poaching on his manor he would punish him, at which Satan appears in a coach drawn by six coal-black steeds. Stephen flees but his wife, Nanny Howe, who was reputed to be a 'witch', strikes out at the Devil with her broomstick. However, she soon submits to his superior power and agrees to go with him.

St Cuthbert's Church, Kildale. According to tradition, on the wooded hilltop above Kildale, an area known as 'Devil's Court', witches congregated under the presidency of their lord and master.

Richard Blakeborough, writing in the 1890s, spoke to elderly Great Ayton folk who were sure they'd seen Nanny Howe riding her broomstick over Howe Wood near to Kildale church in their youth.[18]

A witch-hare story features in a remarkable incident at Scaling on the northern edge of the moors, reported in the *Whitby Gazette* as recently as 1907. The article refers to the destruction by burning of a gigantic old oak tree near the bridge over Greenhow Beck near Scaling Mill, known as Mally (Molly) Harbutt's Tree. It was once the home of Molly Harbutt, a Scots lady, known as the 'witch of the woods', who lived in its large hollow. She prepared potions and was the early equivalent of a homeopathist; she also read fortunes. According to legend she was able to change her shape into a large brown hare, which was finally shot by a hunter, and was subsequently found dying in human form in the branches of the tree. The report in the *Whitby Gazette* states that an old farmer of Scaling, Mr Hutchinson, of Clover Hill Farm, 'recollects quite plainly having personally seen this woman when he was a boy, and he is able to give a very vivid and interesting description of her life'. The tree is marked on maps dating from 1856.

PROTECTION AGAINST WITCHES

With the real fear of 'witches' came methods to protect folk from their powers. Many of us still have a horseshoe nailed to a door or fire surround. Horseshoes were originally made from iron, which was considered magical as it withstood fire, so it was used as a charm to ward off evil spirits.

Witch posts are thought to have been another means of protection from witches. They are a peculiar feature of a number of houses dotted around North Yorkshire, and three examples are held in Ryedale Folk Museum.

Canon Atkinson collected first-hand accounts from his parishioners on how local people protected themselves. It was common to place pieces of rowan

> **SCALING**
> DESTRUCTION BY FIRE OF AN OLD OAK TREE – A fire occurred near Scaling on Saturday night, which destroyed one of the most interesting pieces of scenery in the neighbourhood. This was a magnificent old oak known locally as "Mally Harbutt's Tree," which must have been maliciously set on fire by some ill-disposed person. The fire was observed, about ten o'clock, by a keeper (Mr. Spenceley) and a farmer (Mr. Hugill), who both hastened to the scene, but it was at once apparent that any attempt to stop the fire would be fruitless. These men were shortly afterwards joined by Mr. F. Crosier, the head keeper of Sir Charles Mark Palmer, M.P., upon whose estate the tree stood, and by an under-keeper, who carried buckets to extinguish the flames, if possible. All four men watched the tree until, at about eleven o'clock, it collapsed with a resounding crash, completely destroying a footbridge, which crossed the stream close at hand. The tree was a gigantic oak situated on the bank of a stream between Scaling and Grinkle, and whose bole was hollow to a height of about fifteen or twenty feet. The circumference of the trunk at its base would be about twenty-four feet, and inside the tree about twelve persons could stand at once. Access to the interior could be gained by persons of an arched opening in the trunk. This arch was eight feet in height. The tree is of an enormous age, and was once used as a place of residence by an old witch, or, to be more exact, by a madwoman, for a considerable period. It was from this woman that the tree derived its name, "Mally Harbutt's Tree." An old farmer of Scaling, Mr. Hutchinson, of Clover Hill Farm, recollects quite plainly having personally seen this woman when he was a boy, and he is able to give a very vivid and interesting description of her life. Although the trunk of the tree was only a shell, covered on the inside with a layer of charcoal produced by a previous fire, it was every summer covered with luxuriant foliage. It has been sketched and photographed innumerable times, and it will be mourned for as a personal friend both by the natives and by visitors to the locality.

Transcript of *Whitby Gazette* clipping from 1907.

'Mally (Molly) Harbutt's Tree', Grinkle Woods, before the burning.[19]

Witch Post at Stang End, Ryedale Folk Museum.

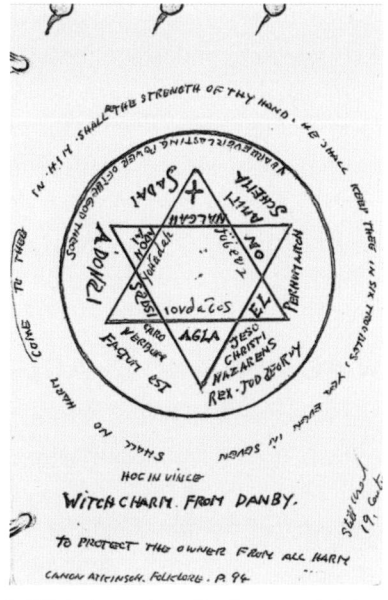

Witch charm from Danby recorded in Bertram Frank's notebook, Ryedale Folk Museum.

wood (known as 'witch-wood') around the house and outbuildings; the wood, in order to become a wood-charm against witches, must be cut on St Helen's day from a tree that the cutter had never seen before, and brought home on a different path from the one used to discover the tree. Atkinson knew an old lady who took measures to expel the 'witch' from her butter churn by sprinkling salt into the fire and into another churn nine times; an alternative method was to sweep the inside of the churn nine times with a red hot poker.

One 'formidable-looking weapon of defence' used to hamper and hinder 'the witch' belonged to a Danby parishioner Atkinson knew personally, a farmer named Jonathan: a 'right good sort, and a fair specimen of the old untutored, unschooled Yorkshire yeoman' with a 'lively sense of the actuality of the witch' and her malice. The charm that Jonathan employed to protect himself and his beasts was found in his bureau following his death, written on a folded and sealed sheet of letter-paper, with 'a hackle from a red cock's neck' inserted between two of the seals.[20] A depiction of this curious witch charm appears in Bert Frank's notebook and is shown in the picture above.

Atkinson notes that 'witch antidotes' and punishments inflicted on witches were generally 'left to inference' rather than 'specified' in the collected witch stories, including 'modes of permanent or sustained annoyance or mortification of the witch'. One example involved a Farndale farmer who had been unlucky with his livestock and had noticed that 'whenivver a lahtle black bitch wur seen i' t' grip o' t' cov-'us, or i' t' calf-pen, then, for seear, yan iv 'em took bad and dee'd.' The black 'female dog' was duly shot with silver shot. The suffering 'witch' was later found in bed with 'a terrible series of shot-wounds'.

WISE MEN AND CHARLATANS

The collected witch stories sometimes talk of victims of witch spells seeking a remedy from a 'Wise Man', who would invariably cast a magical spell that was believed to defeat the witch's power. 'T' Wahse Man o' Stowsley' (Wise Man of Stokesley), a Mr Wrightson, was well known in these parts for making a living as a 'wizard'. He was believed by many to have extraordinary insight, knowledge and power, though some were less convinced.

A 'Yorkshire gentleman' in 1819 is quoted as saying: 'Imposters who feed and live on the superstitions of the lower orders are still to be found in Yorkshire. These are called Wise Men, and are believed to possess the most extraordinary power in remedying all diseases, to discover lost or stolen property, and to foretell future events. One of the wretches was a few years ago living at Stokesley in the North Riding of Yorkshire; his name was John Wrightson … To this fellow people whose education, it might have been expected, would have raised them above such weakness, flocked … All the diseases which he was sought to remedy he invariably imputed to witchcraft…'. Wrightson was accustomed to issuing a drug as a remedy and it was 'always enjoined with some incantation to be observed', and sometimes 'an act of the most wanton barbarity, as that of roasting a game-cock alive, etc'.[21]

Canon Atkinson, though kinder in his estimation of Wrightson, saw him as a charlatan with the 'power of influencing men's minds and imaginations'. Atkinson recorded conversations with John Unthank who, in his youth had visited the Wise Man of Stokesley and found him wearing a long robe and head covering, his consulting room filled with paraphernalia such as a skull, globe and dried herbs. Wrightson's uncanny insight and mesmerising powers, Atkinson deduced, were aided by apprentices who gained knowledge of the wise man's clients prior to consultations, giving Wrightson the appearance of a man with extraordinary prescience.[22]

TELLING THE REAL STORIES OF THE ACCUSED

To step across Blackamoor today, its bare weatherbeaten lonely hills, is to immerse yourself in the echoes of its past. Folklore and a history of oppression and instability buried in its dark roots draws interest from historians, artists, writers, campaigners for oppressed peoples, environmentalists, feminists and today's white witches and herbalists.

The collected stories of local witchcraft around North Yorkshire suggest that moorland communities were still fully immersed in traditions of magic well into the nineteenth century. They hint at a prolonged persecution at village level of vulnerable people branded as 'witches' who were increasingly marginalised in a changing world. Targeted in particular were older women living alone, in poverty, who had been excluded from land work after the land enclosures and were trying to make a living using traditional herbal and magical practices, who were shunned, persecuted and subjected to violence in some cases. Their persecutors experienced a genuine fear of 'witches' and felt justified to make accusations against them and dispense punishments.

At Ryedale Folk Museum researchers are working hard to tell stories of local people accused of witchcraft. If they can tell the stories of the real historic people featured in local witchcraft tales they can avoid the risk of continuing the injustice of portraying them in stories based largely on stereotypes – in the villainous role of the witch in popular culture.

Rosie Barrett at the Museum explains how some of the objects in their collection can help them move closer to knowing these women, though the process is not without difficulty:

'We have evidence of a magic book which belonged to a moorland "witch" known as Peggy Dvell. As well as symbols and spells, it also contains her accumulated "magical" knowledge on plants, flowers and the stars and planets. Often, these objects only add to the confusion as we seek to find a way to understand them whilst rejecting our forebears' use of the label of witch.

'Four "spell tokens" within the collection, dating from the early and mid-eighteenth-century (much later than the intense witch-hunting of the early modern period), are generally interpreted as love 'charms'. These are likely

'Spell tokens' held at Ryedale Folk Museum.

examples of transactional magic, by someone trying to make a living – what historian, Professor Ronald Hutton has termed a "service magician". Adorned with hearts, initials and dates, they speak to us of the desire of women to marry and bear children.'

Martyn Hudson's reflections on Blackamoor bring together a wealth of historical detail, including the lives of the nineteenth-century collectors of witch stories. The George Calvert manuscript, for instance, was commissioned by an obscure antiquary called Martin Stapleton of Ayton. Richard Blakeborough, who found the manuscript and lent it to Bert Frank at the Ryedale Folk Museum, was an antiquary, poet, medic and dramatist who died in active service at the close of the First World War.[23]

Uncovering the secrets of Blackamoor will not be easy. Lack of power and voice of the many moorland women who suffered oppression at the domestic and village level are likely to prevent their stories ever being told. But discovering the true stories of those named in the collectors' records is an essential first step towards challenging stereotypes and stopping injustice for both women in history and those caught up in witch-hunts still happening around the world today.[24]

NICOLA CHALTON

NOTES

1. Blavatsky Collected Writings volume 10, 'Lodges of Magic' by Helena Blavatsky, co-founder of Theosophical Society 1875
2. *On Blackamoor*, Martyn Hudson, TeMeNo Press, 2020
3. www.ryedalefolkmuseum.co.uk
4. Original notebooks of Bert Frank held at Ryedale Folk Museum in which Frank copied by hand the contents of the George Calvert Manuscript.
5. *Forty Years in a Moorland Parish* by Rev. J.C. Atkinson, 1908
6. *Witches in Old North Yorkshire*, Mary Williams, 1987. Percy Shaw Jeffrey (1862–1952) retired to Whitby and wrote *Whitby Lore and Legend* in 1952
7. ibid
8. ibid
9. *Witchcraft, Magic and Culture*, 1736–1951, Owen Davies, 1999
10. *Religion and the Decline of Magic*, Keith Thomas, 1971
11. https://en.wikipedia.org
12. https://en.wikipedia.org/wiki/Witchcraft_Acts
13. British Library Collection item: King James VI and I's *Daemonologie*, 1597
14. *Witch Stories*, E.L. Linton, 1861
15. ibid
16. British Library Medieval manuscripts blog: https://blogs.bl.uk/digitisedmanuscripts/2013/10/anglo-saxon-medicine.html
17. ibid
18. This and similar stories are recorded in *The History and Antiquities of Cleveland* by John Walker Ord (1846), some of which are retold in Mary Williams' book, *Witches in Old North Yorkshire*, 1987
19. Image courtesy of Alan Richardson and the East Cleveland Image Archive (www.image-archive.org.uk); additional information on Molly Harbutt courtesy of Cody McKay
20. p.95, ibid
21. *Observations on the Popular Antiquities of Great Britain Chiefly Illustrating the Origin of Our Vulgar and Provincial Customs, Ceremonies, and Superstitions*, Volume 3, John Brand, Henry Ellis, James Orchard Halliwell-Phillipps, 1849
22. ibid
23. ibid
24. See: 'Witch hunts: A global problem in the 21st century', Charlotte Müller & Sertan Sanderson, August 10, 2020: www.dw.com/en/witch-hunts-a-global-problem-in-the-21st-century/a-54495289

Thank you in particular to Rosie Barrett for access to archive material at Ryedale Folk Museum and her guidance on the presentation of 'The Witch', and to Martyn Hudson for a copy of his book *On Blackamoor*. Also to the East Cleveland Image Archive for use of the rare image of 'Mally (Molly) Harbutt's Tree', Grinkle Woods, and to Caroline Vodden for telling me about it.

Local witches and their attributes according to the Calvert Manuscript

👁 Did also use the evil eye   ☦ Could turn thersels into a cat
✕ Could turn thersels into a hare   ◯ Had a familiar

Nancy Nares o' Pickering 👁 ☦ ⊙ ↔ ☐
Nanny Howe o' Kildale ✕
Nan Hardwicke o' Spittal Houses ✕ ☐
Nanny Newgill o' Broughton ↔ 👁 ⊙
Nanny Pierson o' Goathland ≋
Nan Scaife o' Spaunton Moor
Ann Allan o' Ugthorpe ↔ 👁
Sabina Moss (aka Aud Mother Migg) o' Cropton ⊙
Betty Franks o' Wappley ≋
Sally Craggs o' Allerston ☦ ⊙

≈ Could cripple a quickening bairn ◉ Did use ye crystal
↔ Well up in all matters of the black art □ Used cubes in casting lots

Dina Suggest o' Levisham ○◉
Aud Bett Collet o' Sleights ↔ 👁
Rachel Hesp o' Carlton ✕ □
Hester Mudd o' Rosedale ⊕ 👁
Nan Garbutt o' Great Ayton 👁
Aud Emma Todd o' Ebberston ↔
Leah Biggin o' Stoup Brow ○
Sussanna Price o' Lythe ≈
Lyd Storm o' Ruswarp ✕ 👁 ◉
Elizya Scarthe o' Slingsby 👁 ⊕ □
Megg Peart o' Ellerby ≈ ◉

Moorland Witch Places

Nanny's Nook

Just outside Commondale on the Kildale road, there is a small copse. It hides a double right-angled bend in the dry stone wall called 'Nanny's Nook', said to have been frequented by a witch. This may be Nanny Howe, the witch reputed to have been seen over Great Ayton riding her broomstick just at midnight written about by Richard Blakeborough, the Victorian scholar of Yorkshire folklore.

The 1853 Ordnance Survey map does not name Nanny's Nook, but it does name, 300 metres away, Nanny's Spring.[1]

Nanny Howe

A Bronze Age burial mound known as 'Nanny Howe' is one of a group of several tumuli on the wooded hilltop of Coate Moor,[2] half a mile east from Captain Cook's monument which stands above Great Ayton. The site features in Frank Elgee's archaeological survey of the 1930s and was described by Elgee as associated with a prehistoric settlement and also folklore. Elgee and his wife wrote that the site as a whole was known as 'Devil's Court where, according to tradition, witches congregated under the presidency of their lord and master'.[3]

The folklorist and historian Richard Blakeborough elaborates:

'Again, old people of Great Ayton still aver that on a certain night a once-noted witch, Nanny Howe, may be seen riding astride on a broomstick over Howe Wood just at midnight. This witch, so mounted, is said once to have chased the devil for miles – on this occasion the two must have fallen out; perhaps at that time honest folk got their due. Howe Wood is near Kildale.'[4]

MICK GARRATT

---

1 Photo and information courtesy of Mike Garratt, www.fhithich.uk, 17 Oct 2020
2 OS Grid Reference NZ 599 103
3 *The Archaeology of Yorkshire*, Frank & Harriet Elgee, 1933
4 *Wit, Character, Folklore and Customs of the North Riding of Yorkshire*, Richard Blakeborough, 1911

The 'Witch' from Marske

Richard Blackborough, the Stockton-based folklorist, wrote in 1898:

Peggy Flaunders died in 1835, at the age of eighty-five, and was buried in the churchyard at Marske-by-the-Sea. Many old people have a lively remembrance of Peggy, with her tall hat and red cloak; and the stories which are told today of the pranks she played and the wonders she worked, make us open our eyes with amazement, because we are not listening to the marvellous deeds of some person who lived in mediaeval times, but of one who lived amongst those now living. Do you wish to hear of her doings from one who knew her? Then find your way to Boyes Wetherell's cottage, and have a chat with the old worthy, and you will have such an outpouring of ancient customs, rites, lore, smuggling stories, and the doings of days gone by, together with touches of his own eventful life, as will stock your mind with information such as it is only possible to obtain from an original source.[1]

But of Peggy and her doings. On one occasion Peggy is said to have cast a spell against one Tom Pearson (who lived on a farm near Marske), and every head of cattle he possessed died. Whether this ruined him or not, is not known, but he left the farm, and his cousin took it. As this cousin crossed the threshold for the first time, Peggy passed by. (This cousin, it seems, had once befriended Peggy.) She called out to him as she passed, 'Thoo 'ez mah good wishes,' and with that she turned three times round, threw her cloak on the ground, jumped over it, mumbled something, and walked away, and from that day everything prospered 'awlus wiv him'.[2]

---

1   Boyes Wetherell lost his wife on the birth of their first child, a boy. Boyes tended his bairn with a mother's love and care, and when the child was four years old, he tramped all the way to London with the lad on his back. Once they slept in a grave. But that's another story!
2   *Wit, Character, Folklore and Customs of the North Riding of Yorkshire*, Richard Blakeborough, 1911

Witch's Broom

◆ Where does the stereotypical image of a witch flying on a broomstick come from?

Brooms were traditionally associated with women and their domestic tasks, and yet the first record of a 'witch' confessing to riding a broom was a man: Guillaume Edelin, an Augustinian and Doctor of Divinity arrested in 1453 for promoting the idea that it was impossible for witches to fly on brooms or make pacts with the Devil. He was imprisoned for life after confessing under torture.

The first known illustration depicting women riding broomsticks is in the margin of a fifteenth-century manuscript featuring a poem by Martin Le Franc, 'Le Champion des Dames', written in defence of virtuous women. The image depicts two Waldensians – identified by their headscarves. Waldensians were branded heretics by the Catholic Church in 1215, for threatening Church authority and allowing preaching and consecration of the sacrament by any layperson, including women. They were subjected to intense persecution for two centuries.[1]

---

1   *Feminae: Medieval Women and Gender Index* – 'Two Waldensian Witches': https://inpress.lib.uiowa.edu/feminae

The Curious Case of the Region's 'Witch Posts'

Around a number of houses in North-East Yorkshire, predominantly in the North York Moors, there can be found puzzling wooden posts. Known nowadays as 'witch posts', approximately twenty-five are known to survive, with a few examples in the Yorkshire Dales and neighbouring Lancashire. But what are they? And why are they here?

The most commonly-accepted interpretation is that they were believed to protect the house or hearth from evil, perhaps even the influence of witches. The X-shaped St Andrew's cross adorning the posts is therefore generally viewed as an apotropaic symbol. Most people will be familiar with superstitions surrounding the impulse to cross – we still cross our fingers for good luck and mark hot-cross buns, nowadays for tradition's sake but once upon a time for protection.

Apotropaic markings speak of the fears that were once widespread, particularly between the sixteenth and eighteenth centuries. Protective marks were often placed near doors, windows and chimneys.

Ryedale Folk Museum has three posts within the collection, including one in situ inside 'Stang End', a seventeenth-century cruck-framed cottage which was relocated to the museum from the nearby village of Danby. Posts can also be found at Whitby Museum and Pitt Rivers Museum, Oxford.

Positioned near the fireplace, the carved posts were possibly believed to prevent evil from entering through the chimney. King James's *Daemonologie* – his treatise on necromancy, magic and the occult written in 1597 – identified the importance of protecting the hearth from witches' familiars, claiming: 'they will come and pierce through, whatever house or church, though all ordinary passages be closed', specifically gaining access through any opening 'the air may enter in at'.

The post in Stang End also hides a silver threepenny bit. One story tells that when the cream was 'witched' and wouldn't churn into butter, the threepenny bit should be carefully dug out from its hiding place and dropped in the pail.

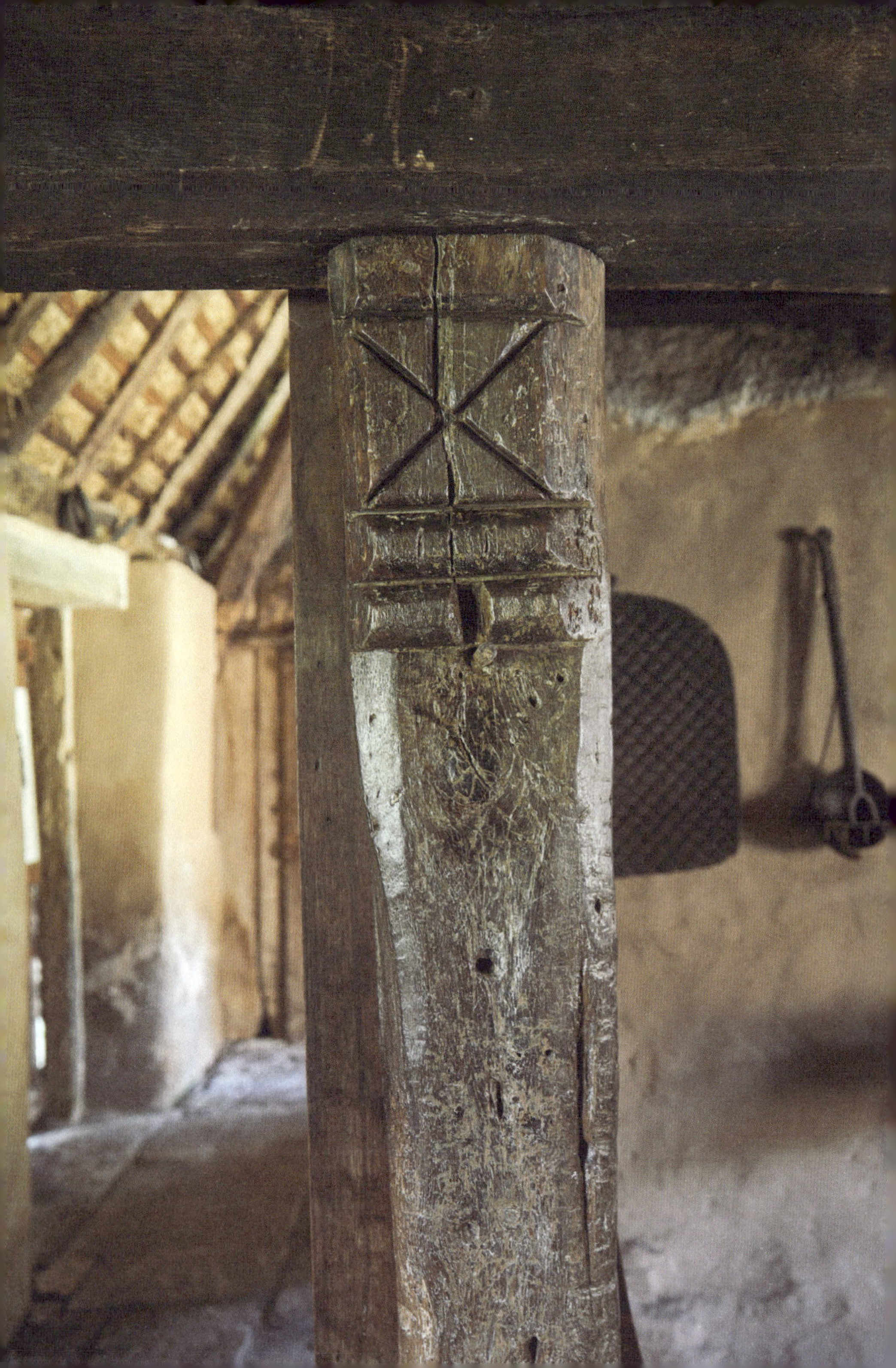

Witch post at 'Stang End'.

A further 'witch post', originally from the nearby village of Gillamoor and currently in store at the Museum, held a selection of curious items – a coil of sheep's wool and a piece of blue calico, but no coin. Two further grooves in the wood reveal carefully-snipped sprigs of horse hair.

Ritualistic steps to keep evil away from the home or outbuildings weren't unusual: a single boot ensconced within a thatched roof; a horseshoe above the door; a rowan tree planted nearby. There are also several 'hag stones' on display at Ryedale Folk Museum, rocks or pebbles with naturally-occurring holes, favoured for their purported magical properties.

From the late eighteenth-century onwards it seems that the 'witch posts' had lost their significance and some may have been taken out during rebuilding, sometimes reused as lintels. Nowadays, questions remain and their ritualistic markings and embellishments are not widely understood. The geographical clustering around the North York Moors is additionally intriguing. Why here, in this pocket of North Yorkshire?

ROSIE BARRETT

Protective Markings – X Marks the Spot!

A carved knitting sheath.

Across the world, old homes bear the marks of history. In some cases, these were deliberately made as part of a system of house protection through magical means. Often they were scratched, burned and carved into the fabric of buildings, possibly during rituals.

These deliberate symbols, including daisy wheels or hexafoils, criss-crossings and meshes, have been often regarded as historic graffiti. Unfortunately, they are sometimes passed over by building surveyors for this reason.

A surprising number of everyday objects in the collection at Ryedale Folk Museum were also deliberately marked. This gives us clues about the parts of life where our ancestors felt most vulnerable.

Probably the most common protective mark was the diagonal cross, or X. The idea of crossing has remained connected with protection in our modern thinking. We still cross our fingers for good luck and mark hot cross buns at Easter.

As well as marking our 'witch posts', it can be found on everything from apple scoops to knitting sheaths. By the seventeenth century, handknitting was conducted using a curved metal needle. This was held in place between the right hand and a sheath secured at the side of the body. Many museum collections have decorated knitting sheaths in their collections which vary in design according to region – however, they often feature protective markings and also hearts. Most sheaths were not made by professional woodworkers. In fact, they were frequently carved as love tokens by young men for their intended brides.

ROSIE BARRETT

© Ryedale Folk Museum

Concealed Objects Hidden Across Homes

Our ancestors feared not only witches and their familiars, but also fire and accidents, famine and intruders. To avert a range of supernatural threats and natural dangers, they concealed objects believed to convey protection around their homes. Such 'superstitious' activities are known to have happened from medieval times into the nineteenth century, and occasionally even beyond.

Popular locations for concealment included openings and portals like the hearth, as well as doorways, thresholds, and any void spaces, including in roofs and behind walls.

The most commonly-concealed objects seem to have been shoes. Across the country, lots of museum collections contain such items, once belonging to both adults and children, but it's likely that many concealed shoes found during house renovations have been thrown away without the finder knowing their significance.

However, when correctly identified, today's inhabitants sometimes choose to return concealed objects to where they were found, perhaps feeling a little superstitious themselves at the thought of removing the objects and leaving their houses exposed! Others give them to their local museum, like the pair of mid-nineteenth century shoes from Bishopthorpe in York Museums Trust's collection. Over at The Folly in Settle, where the Museum of North Craven Life is based, two shoes (not a pair) concealed within in the building itself are now part of the museum collection.

Since shoes bear an imprint from the wearer, they may have been thought to act as a substitute for them too. Another possible theory is that when placed around the chimney or building perimeter, perhaps shoes served as decoys for harmful forces.

Another, even stranger concealment was that of dried cats, occasionally described as 'mummified'. This term has been used because the cats sometimes dried out very slowly, becoming shrivelled and taking on the appearance of being mummified. Cats have long been associated with magic and witchcraft, but they were also valued for their skills in keeping the vermin population in check. Some cats are even known to have been posed in the process of hunting, suggesting that they might have been thought to have a supernatural ability in the afterlife.

We know of several examples of mummified cats being found in Yorkshire, including in Kirkbymoorside, Whitby, Easingwold and York.

| Witch bottle, before being reconcealed.

Another regularly-concealed object that must be acknowledged is the 'witch bottle', about which more is known than many other objects, with records dating from the seventeenth century. Mostly they were found in the vicinity of the hearth.

Created within stoneware or glass bottles, these vessels were thought to hold counter-spells against witchcraft and were also part of folk-healing methods, often resorted to by people afflicted with illness. Early witch bottles were often made from the widely-imported German 'bartmann' stoneware. They are known as 'bellarmines' due to their resemblance to Cardinal Bellarmine, known for his anti-Protestantism.

Almost 250 have been identified in England, almost all containing either iron pins or nails. Notably, iron has been regarded as a magical metal feared by fairies and witches.

ROSIE BARRETT

♦ If you find items in your own home, you can report them to become part of a database at www.apotropaios.co.uk. Ryedale Folk Museum have been working with the author of *Magical House Protection: The Archaeology of Counter-Witchcraft*, Brian Hoggard, to find out more about objects from the North York Moors.

A Concealed Spoon at Harome Hall - But Why?

Ryedale Folk Museum's re-constructed Harome Hall was the home of a concealed object of some significance – though it will never be known for certain if its concealment was for protective purposes or not. In 1971, when the building was being dismantled to transfer from Harome to Hutton-le-Hole, a silver spoon was found tucked away within the thatch.

A spoon would have been considered an appropriate object for protection due to its intimate connection with a homeowner, literally entering the person through the mouth. Because spoons often feature among groups of other concealed protective objects, there is little doubt that they were thought to have a protective function. One was found, for example, in the West Midlands with a shoe.

Other evidence that might appear to corroborate this superstitious concealment is that Harome Hall also has protective daisy wheels on one of the door frames, showing that magical thinking was afoot during some points in the building's history.

During feudal times, except for the village church, a manor house was generally the most important building in the area. Archaeological evidence shows that the hall's original site in Harome had hosted an important dwelling for eight hundred years.

However, by the 1970s things looked a little different. The hall was described by Museum volunteers as 'crumbling'. The thatch was rotten and the roof collapsing. A rescue plan was put in place. One of the Museum's early trustees, Bill Goodall, arranged for Harome Hall to be removed to the Museum where it would be rebuilt in its 'original simplicity'.

It was volunteer Robin Butler who found the spoon on 17 January 1971. Initially, it seemed to be quite insignificant and was assumed to be made of tin or pewter. For some days the spoon lay in the 'Finds' Tray, along with various pieces of pottery, before a gentle clean revealed a silver hallmark.

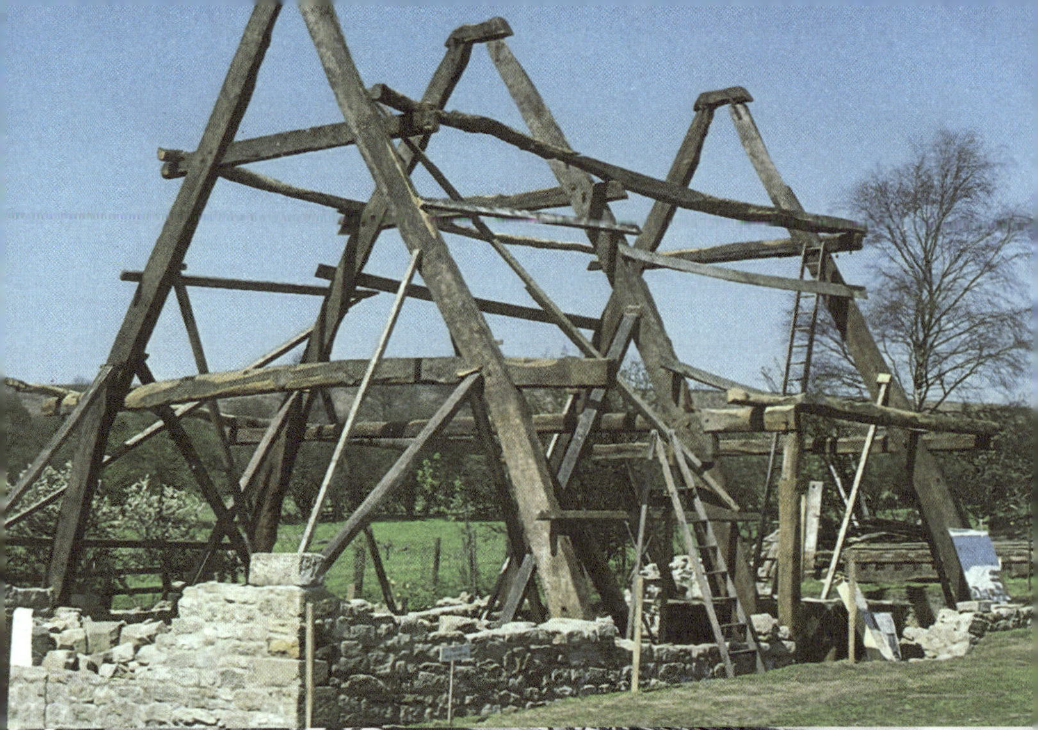

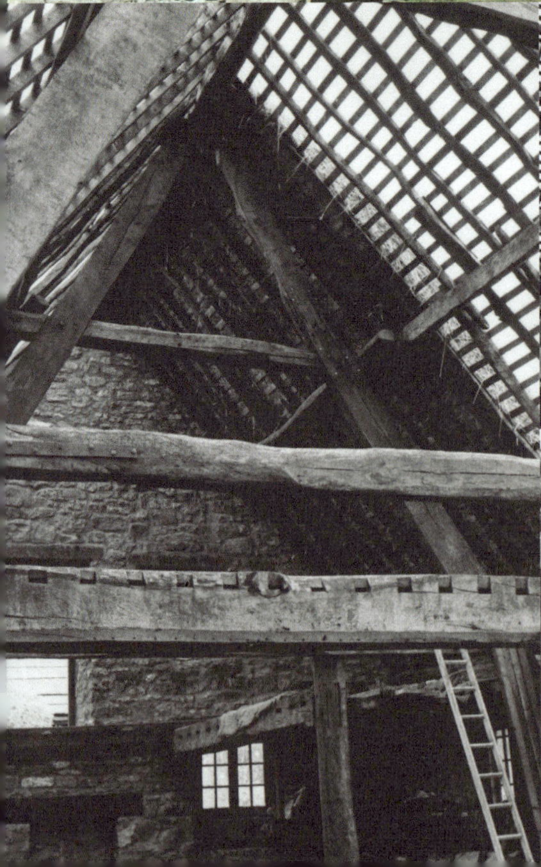

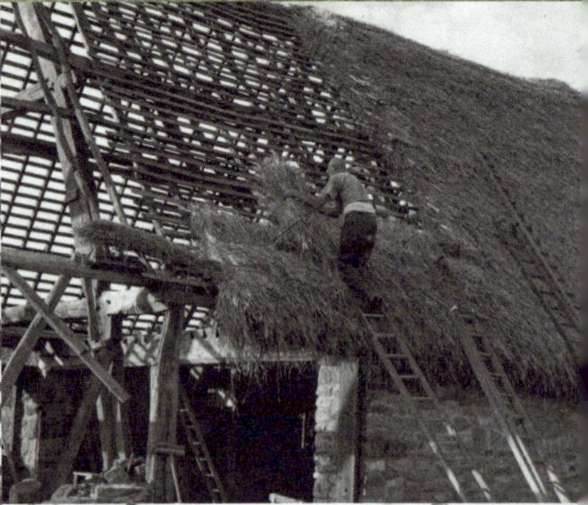

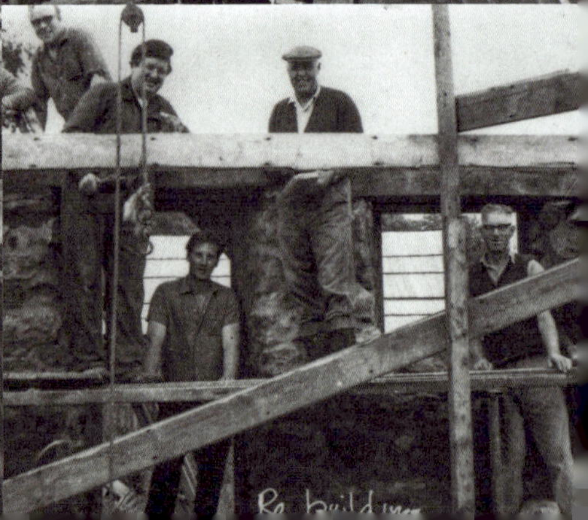

The spoon was now also a candidate for 'treasure trove'. This is the label applied when a hidden item of treasure is too old for the heirs to be traced. In fact, the spoon is now known to have been made in 1510. At the time, producing a silver spoon would have been an indicator of social status, particularly if those about you were using more common wooden spoons.

It is a beautiful piece, measuring approximately fifteen centimetres in length. Its shallow, fig-shaped bowl is in keeping with its intended use for general eating, rather than for liquids as we might use a spoon today. This bowl tapers into a hexagonal stem, ending with a finial knop. Could such a special object really have been concealed for protection?

Another theory relates to the English Civil War, during which Helmsley Castle was besieged in 1644 by Sir Thomas Fairfax. The Royalists held on for three months before surrendering. It is possible that the spoon was concealed at that time by the Hall's inhabitant, the widowed Mary Morrett, to prevent it being stolen by Oliver Cromwell's 'Roundheads', led by Sir Fairfax. They would have been frequent visitors to the villages surrounding Helmsley in search of supplies during the siege.

It's most likely that we'll never be certain of the reason why the Harome Hall spoon was concealed – or if either theory is correct.

ROSIE BARRETT

| Opposite: rebuilding Harome Hall at Hutton-le-Hole.

Folk Healing and Magical Thinking

For much of history, illness must have been a source of terror for most people, with formal medicines out of reach due to the costs. This may have made little difference to the outcomes of the sickly and suffering, however. During the seventeenth century, physicians preached that illness sprang from an imbalance between the four humours in the body (blood, phlegm, yellow bile and black bile). They prescribed potions, lotions and blood-letting accordingly, with very limited understanding of how to treat most illnesses.

For the poor, without access to physicians, medicine tended to begin at home. Housewives had their own tried and tested techniques, based on knowledge of plants and herbs, which would have been passed down the generations. In times of particular need, however, such methods would have needed supplementary help from a wise woman or wise man.

These 'specialists' offered a whole range of services as well as healing, making use of charms, spells, prayers and other remedies. Within rural areas, such healers tended to be some of the humblest members of society, depending upon their fees for survival and sometimes falling under the label of 'witch'.

Betty Strother, who lived 'ower by Castleton' and is known to have died an old lady in 1775, was viewed as a sorceress, skilled in white magic, and was well-visited for her cures for both humans and animals. There were also known to be 'wise men' at Byland, Kilburn, Nunnington, Helmsley, Kirkbymoorside, Lastingham, Cropton and Helmsley. The best known of all, however, was the Wise Man of Stokesley, John Wrightston – as well as curing illness, he was also able to locate stolen goods!

Charms featured heavily within folk healing, but, ephemeral in nature due to their basis in natural materials, they are rare within museum collections. Scarborough Museums and Galleries has a collection of charms, however, thanks to the personal passions of naturalist William Clarke.

Born in Scarborough in 1868, Clarke developed an early interest in the natural world, later becoming a founding member of the Scarborough Field

© Angela Waites Photography

Naturalists. Clarke's notebooks, documenting instances of folk belief, also provide valuable insights into the persistence of magical practices and beliefs into the early 1900s.

The Clarke Charm Collection ranges from charms for curing ailments and bringing luck, to amulets providing protection against negative forces. Many show examples of folklore drawing inspiration from nature for healing purposes and are frequently based on magical thinking, such as the skin of an eel which was worn above the knee as a charm against cramp, apparently for over 20 years, by Mrs W.E. Hemsley of Filey.

Though many charms appear far-fetched, it is now understood that when we believe a treatment will help, the human mind is able to trigger real, physiological changes in the body, leading to improvements in symptoms known as 'the Placebo Effect'. It seems likely that this was at work when charm-wearers and carriers insisted on their healing effects!

ROSIE BARRETT

Herbal Wisdom of the Past: Moorland Dew

I have always been fascinated by the herbal health properties of our wild flora, making tonic teas from sage and ground ivy by the time I was nine or ten, learning from my mother and grandmother. I have used them carefully and successfully ever since: making me a 'green' or 'hedge' witch in the eyes of some!

From our early beginnings, we humans have used wild plants and trees for health and healing, as many animals do too. At first, the information was probably gathered by intuition or trial and error, spreading by imitation, then by word of mouth between close family and friendship groups. The knowledge became more refined and the specific skills were shared wider and written down.

As this knowledge became more useful, it also brought prestige, power and payment. And so it became more closely guarded, often within religious or professional societies. Written in Greek or Latin, it then became unavailable to the poorer people without education.

But in parallel to this were the 'wise women' in many societies, who quietly learnt and absorbed the wisdom and practised herbal medicine in their communities, keeping a low profile to prevent accusations of witchcraft and subsequent ducking or death. Knowledge and power were jealously guarded! Even now, as gradually the plant chemicals of their remedies have been recognised, isolated and synthesised to make our modern pharmacy, competition has not been completely replaced by cooperation!

So my botanical curiosity was piqued when a local friend gave me this little 'poem' from the past to explain… if I could!

From the *Widdowes Treasure*: a book of home remedies written by John Partridge and first published in 1595:[1]

This decoction is good to eat
Always before and after meat
For it will make digestion good
And turn your meat into pure blood
Besides all this it doth excell
All windinesie for to expell
And all gross humours cold and raw
That are in belly, stomack, maw
It will dissolve without paine
And keep ill vapours from the braine
Beside all this it will restore
Your memory though lost before.
Use it therefore when you please,
Therein resteth mighty ease.

There was a note that the decoction might be Rosa solis cordial. My initial research showed that this was a favourite cordial of the time, having a reputation for being a great strengthening and nourishing tonic, even an aphrodisiac, as well as a cure for various health problems. All over Europe it was drunk in company, convivially as we do with coffee now. It was alcohol based with various herbs and spices, but always one specific ingredient: 'Rosa solis'.

Further investigation indicated that this name had nothing to do with roses, but should read Ros-solis. Deriving from the Latin '*ros*' meaning dew, or '*rosea*' meaning dewy, and '*solis*' the sun, it refers to the plant we know as Sundew (*Drosera rotundifolia*) – '*drosos*' also being Greek for dew! This is a carnivorous species of flowering plant of high acidic sphagnum bogs and moorland flushes, growing in abundance on the North York Moors in such areas, though absent from drier, heather-dominated places. The leaves, in a low basal rosette, are round and stalked with red glandular hairs on their upper surfaces that are tipped with a sticky liquid. This liquid attracts, entraps and then dissolves insects as the leaf curls around them.

In the past, those who practised herbal medicine traditionally picked most herbs when the dew was still on them; a plant that was always dew-covered was considered special, even magical! Unbeknown to them, this 'dew' on

Sundew (*Drosera rotundifolia*) contained chemicals – enzymes – that could break down proteins, dissolving the insects that they caught, providing the plant with the extra nutrients needed to survive in such acidic, poor environments: a carnivorous plant!

How satisfying it was, as a botanist, to realise the possibility that a decoction of the plant, preserved in alcohol, could break down the proteins in meat – a large part of the diet then – to 'make digestion good'.

The possibility then occurred to me that the latter half of the poem, 'It will restore, Your memory though lost before', could suggest that the decoction may also digest the tangled amyloid proteins in the brain, that we now believe are heavily involved in the development of dementia.

Imagine what other powerful herbal wisdom lies in the knowledge of the people of the past on our moorland doorstep today.

ANNE PRESS

1   British Library Collection: www.bl.uk/collection-items/the-widdowes-treasure

2

FAIRIES, CREATURES, GHOSTS & LEGENDS

Lealholm Hob
Hob o' Thrush
T'Hob o' Hobgarth
Cross Hob o' Lastingham
Farndale Hob o' High Farndale
Elphi o' Low Farndale
Scugdale Hob
Hodge Hob o' Bransdale
Wood Howe Hob
T'Hob o' Brackken Howe
T'Hob o' Stummer Howe
T'Hob o' Tarn Hole
Hob o' Ankness
Crookelby Hob
Hob o' Hasty Bank
T'Hob o' Chop Yate
Blea Hob
T'Hob o' Broxa
T'Hob o' Pye Rigg
Goathland Hob o' Howlmoor
T'Hob o' Egton High Moor

Hobs of the North York Moors

Nowadays, we are very fortunate to have magical helpers in our lives. Each year, Father Christmas appears in this country during the early hours of Christmas day morning. Another well-known magical visitor is the tooth fairy, who is welcomed into many homes throughout the year. But in the past, people of the North York Moors also had 'hobs' to help them, if they were lucky.

Sometimes called 'hobgoblins', hobs were a type of fairy folk that included house elves and farm elves, although in these parts the word elf was more commonly understood to be referring to the 'wicked' little people, whilst hobs were frequently helpful.

Hobs were once believed to live in many homes in the North York Moors and their name still appears in placenames on maps of the region. In the 1820s, George Calvert was concerned that the names of hobs who were commonly held to live in the North York Moors region should be recorded before they were lost. He compiled a list based on the stories he had been told and recorded it in the Calvert Manuscript.

ROSIE BARRETT

Hobs, Goblins, Boggles and Sprites

◆ From the moorland areas of North Yorkshire, especially the far north-east corner and along the craggy coastal strip, come numerous folktales and legends, many of them involving supernatural beings called hobs. Their kin are found in folklore throughout Northern England and Scotland, and go by various names including hobs, goblins, boggles, boggarts and sprites.

Hobs are elf-like creatures that are rarely, if ever, seen. Their existence is only confirmed by evidence left behind from their activities. They are said to be shaggy, ugly little fellows with coarse and scanty clothing, if any. However, to offer them new clothing would be deeply upsetting to them. If left alone, they are generally benign and helpful creatures, performing good deeds in the night. Except, that is, when they are offended. Then they can turn malicious and cause untold mischief and mayhem. You must never offend a hob.

Hob Hole near Westerdale.

Hob Holes or caves in the cliffs of Runswick Bay were left from jet mining. A hob was reputed to live there.

Hobs are usually associated with a specific location or local habitat. For instance there is a so-called Hob's Cave at Mulgrave, Sandsend. Also a legend of the Hob of Hart Hall Farm, Glaisdale, about a very industrious sprite or goblin that carried out winnowing and harrowing and other farm chores to assist the hard-pressed farmer with his workload.

The water splash and beck-side picnic spot on the road from Westerdale to Kildale known as Hob Hole was no doubt once the home of a hob, or still is? And likewise at Boggle Hole, Robin Hood's Bay – boggle being another name for a hob. Beware, there are hobs everywhere.

At Runswick Bay a legend surrounds a dark cave called Hob Hole, where the resident hob became famous for its magical power to cure children of the kink-cough (whooping cough), or so it was believed. Children suffering from the disease were escorted to the mouth of the cave where the accompanying adult would invoke the cure by calling out to the hob, deep inside the cave, the short incantation:

'Hob-hole hob! Mah bairn's gotten the kink-cough;

Tak' it off, tak' it off!'

It is not known whether this strange remedy actually worked.

THE FARNDALE HOB

Perhaps the most widespread and well-known story is that of the notorious Farndale Hob. This 'spirit' had helped with laborious work on a farm in Farndale for at least two generations. When the old farmer died he was succeeded by his hard-working son who continued to tend the animals and improve the land with the mysterious overnight help of the resident hob. The farm prospered. The farmer and his young wife greatly appreciated the clandestine help from the hob despite the unsettling noise and disturbance it created in the night. As a small token of their appreciation, each evening they left out a jug of fresh cream. Every morning the jug was empty, although the hob was never seen.

Unfortunately tragedy struck; the kindly farmer's wife took ill and died. The farmer struggled on but was lonely and eventually remarried. The new wife, however, was mean and curmudgeonly. Berating her husband for his extravagant gift to the hob of a jug of fresh cream each night, she substituted it for skimmed milk or water. We can only assume that the hob was greatly offended as from that day on things went badly on the farm.

Farndale, home of the Farndale Hob

The hob immediately ceased doing his valuable overnight work. The hens stopped laying. The farmhorse went lame. The cows' milk yield plummeted. A fox killed the geese. The butter went rancid. The crops failed. Mishap followed mishap as the stoic farmer struggled on. On top of all this, the house and outbuildings became haunted. Strange and frightening disturbances occurred through the night. Eerie screams were heard, covers and sheets were pulled off beds by unseen hands. No farmhand or maidservant would stay and the farmer and his wife could not sleep. They believed the hob had turned into an evil spirit and resolved to exorcise it, but all attempts were in vain. The mayhem continued. The sudden death of their prized sow was the last straw. Reluctantly the couple decided they had no alternative but to up-sticks and leave the ill-fated farmstead – and their troubles – behind.

They found a vacant farmstead a few miles away and laboriously moved all their farm-stock and equipment over several days. On the final day, they came back for the last load of household furniture. The farmer drove carefully down the rough track, his wife keeping a watchful eye on the cart piled high with chairs and stools, feather beds, lamps, brooms, copperware and other household items. A little way down the track they met a neighbour. *'Hello,'* he called out cheerily, *'What are ye about? Where are ye gannin?'*

'We are flitting,' came the farmer's sad reply. At that, there came a strange husky voice, *'Aye, we're flitting!'* it called out loudly. The shocked farmer and his wife turned to see at the rear of their cart a frightful wizened ugly figure, grinning, his black eyes flashing with malicious glee . . .

For a moment the startled farmer froze with fear. Then with an air of desperation he resigned and called out, *'Well, if thou art flitting with us, we may as well flit back again!'*

And so, it is said, the distraught farmer and his wife returned to their old abode. It is not known what the future held for them, or if the hob relented and behaved himself thereafter. But the lesson is clear – never offend a hob!

AINSLEY

The Hob Song

I hang things up, collect the eggs
I scrub and wash, I make the beds,
I shine the shoes, I sweep and clean,
All I want, All I want, All I want,
Is a spot of cream...

I milk the cows, I sheer the sheep,
I wind the yarn, all while you sleep,
I weave and knit, and fix the seams,
All I want, All I want, All I want...
Is a spot of cream...

Cream for my supper, smooth as silk
The richest, dreamiest top of the milk,
When it comes to cream I'm a pussy cat,
It keeps me hale and hearty and fat,
Give me cream, that's just the job!
Just a spot of cream and I'm a happy hob!

I rake the hay, I grease the plough,
The chores all done, you don't know how
I work all night, unheard, unseen,
All I want,
All I want,
All I want...
Is a spot of cream...

OR WHAT
IS THIS DISGUSTING GRUEL
IT'S THIN AND PALE AND WEAK AND COOL,
MUST I ACCEPT THIS RIDICULE?
HOW DARE YOU TAKE ME FOR A FOOL!

I'll smash the glass, kick down the door,
I'll dump the pigswill on the floor,
I'll pour this milk down your latrine -
All I want, All I want, All I want...

Is a spot of cream!

HAZEL GOULD

The Hobman of Upleatham

Upleatham Old Church was once referred to as 'the smallest church in England' – a superlative that is usually disputed but which, as far as I know, has never been refuted.

However, it is not this quaint little church which concerns me here but a small hill just over a mile to the north east, slap bang in the middle of Saltburn Golf Course – Hob Hill.

There are folk tales about hobs, those little impish creatures, in many remote dales of the North York Moors. Not so many though in the Tees Valley. In several of these folk tales, the hob, initially helping a poor overworked farmer, takes offence and begins to cause trouble. The farmer and his family resolve to flit (or move), and the hob declares his determination of going with them to their new abode. But in this story from Upleatham, the hob is driven away, and it is this departure which gives a witch a chance for revenge against the farmer. Richard Blakeborough recounted the story in the *Northern Weekly Gazette*, 1902:[1]

'At one time there lived a Hobman in Hob Hill, near Upleatham, who seems to have been a blessing to a farmer named Oughtred. It was no uncommon thing for this man to have his corn thrashed and winnowed during the night by the Hob, and when things were a bit hard pushed, unseen by anyone, the Hob turned to with a will, attending to and completing all manner of odd jobs – such as bringing the kie[2] to be milked, gathering eldin[3] together, etc, etc. But, unfortunately, one of the farm lads, when leaving the barn, forgot to bring away his jacket, which he had tossed over a cart end, so that when the Hobman entered, intending to do a few good turns for the farmer, his eye fell upon the jacket; and, no doubt, thinking that Oughtred had left it there as a present for him, took instant offence, for nothing so offended the Hobs as to have wearing apparel of any kind offered to them. Nay, it would seem as though they objected to presents or bribes at any time. So hurt was the Hobman on finding the jacket, that he went away there and then, and was never heard of again.

I want the reader to carefully keep in mind this last quotation. No sooner was the Hobman thus driven away than a witch, living at Marske-by-Sea, one Peggy Flaunders, or Flinders, seized the opportunity of paying off an old score which she had, or fancied she had, against the Oughtreds. Evidence of her ill will was soon forthcoming. Very shortly after the departure of the Hobman there came one night towards bedtime a knock at the kitchen door. The maid, on opening it, stood dumbfounded and flabbergasted; trembling, she stood with her eyes almost out of her head with fear, but for the moment speechless. And well she might be, and so would the bravest of us had we beheld standing within a foot of us a fearful apparition, a creature fearful to behold, the like of which she had never seen before, and which she afterwards declared to be 'T' maist like a blazing pig ov owt'.

At last the girl gave one wild shriek, and rushed into the room in which her master and mistress were seated. The moment they really understood from the affrighted maid what had happened, they at once begged her to calm herself, and say whether she had closed the house door before rushing into their presence?

'Neea, mistress', hysterically sobbed the lass. 'Ah shut now't. Ah war ti skart ti ho'd my wits. Ah did now't bud skrike cot an' tak my skite. Ah shut now't, neea marry nut Ah.'

When the Oughtreds heard that the back door had been thus deserted and left open, they shook their heads, and, overcome with the ill news, they both sank back upon the settle filled with fear, well knowing that the evil spirit would not fail to seize such an opportunity of entering and so gaining a lodgment in their house. Sure enough such was the case; from that night ill luck fell upon all their endeavours. Crops were ruined, stock died, their crockery was thrown upon the floor, until at last things got into such a parlous state that they decided upon leaving the place and seeking pastures new.

The night preceding the day upon which they were to remove their belongings, a friend looked in.

'Whya whah them, thoo's riddy fer off, is ta?' questioned the caller. But before Oughtred could make reply a queer little head, with pointed ears, popped in sight from above the press, and a little, squeaking voice made answer:

'Ay, we're gahin' ti flit ti morn at morn.'

On hearing this Oughtred, in a tone fairly wrung with despair, said, 'Oha, if that be t'case it's ti neea use flitting at all. If thoo's gahin' an' all wa mud just ez weel bide wheear wa be.' And the story says that they did not shift.

Oughtred, it seems, sought out some wise man, and by him was told to pierce with pins and roast alive a live cock bird at dead of night, with closed doors, windows and every key hole and cranny carefully fastened and stopped up. This having been successfully carried out in every detail, Peggy's evil spell was broken, and the evil spirit for over banished.'

So, if you happen to be playing on Saltburn Golf Course and mess up a shot, you will now have the perfect excuse.

MICK GARRATT

---

1   'Hobmen or Brownies', Blakeborough, R., *Northern Weekly Gazette*, Saturday 29 November, 1902, British Newspaper Archive, britishnewspaperarchive.co.uk
2   Cows
3   Fuel, especially peat, turfs, sticks, brushwood, etc

Handale Priory

Handale Priory (also known as Grendale Priory) near Loftus, was founded in 1133 as a small nunnery. Its exact position is unknown but is likely to have been close to Handale's eighteenth-century Grade II listed walled garden, which contains recycled medieval masonry.

It is said that nuns from Rosedale Abbey journeyed to Handale as penance, the route being long and arduous.

After the Reformation the Priory mill was used for the manufacture of cotton garments, and in the eighteenth century the Priory ruins were incorporated into the farmhouse and walled garden that you can see today.

Evidence of Handale Priory can also be seen in the medieval fish pond to the south of the walled garden and the medieval tomb lid and cross base, both relocated to the base of a medieval wall adjacent to the farmhouse.

A circular walk from Loftus to Handale Abbey can be found at: www.walkingloftusandthenorthyorkshirecoast.com/self-guided-walks

The Tale of the Handale Wyrm

Dragon lore is not uncommon in North Yorkshire. Our local dragons are generally called 'worms' from the Old English 'wyrm' and Old Norse 'ormr', meaning snake or serpent.

Handale is a couple of miles south of Loftus and during the twelfth century was describes a fire-breathing worm who had a taste for the beautiful maids of Loftus. The beast would lure them into its lair and keep them there for several days before eating them.

This retelling by Helen Atkinson was designed as a verbal account for children at a Heritage Open Day event; the children then finger-knitted a wyrm as part of the event.

Once upon a time, a long time ago, but very close to us in Handale Woods, a serpent hatched in a cave. Now this was not just any type of snake, it was a magical, mythical wyrm who would grow to be twenty feet long, with a poisonous venom and the ability to breathe fire! You wouldn't have known that when he was born, however, as it just appeared to be a normal snake.

As the wyrm grew bigger and bigger it started to get the taste for something with more substance than the mice it could find in the woods. It started to slither onto the farms in Handale, Loftus and Liverton to steal their chickens. The farmers did not notice the wyrm as it was very clever and only came in the dead of night, which made them think that it was a fox who was stealing all the chickens and all the eggs. All of this food meant that the serpent grew even bigger and chickens were not enough for it anymore! Soon it started to take other animals from the local farms like the sheep and the goats, even the occasional pig. This was a bit more worrying for the local people as it clearly was something larger than a fox that was stealing all of their livestock! But still, they could not catch the creature nor figure out what it was so could not do anything about it.

After a few months of the sheep and goats being stolen (and eaten!), the farmers decided that something must be done. Overnight they started to lock away their animals in their barns so that nothing could get to them. This angered the wyrm greatly as he could no longer eat so he hatched a plan to punish the farmers who had locked up their animals. He decided that he would slither in through the windows of their houses and steal away their daughters in the middle of the night! Overall he took sixteen young maidens and trapped them in his cave.

Of course, all who were trapped were terrified! It was dark, it was damp, it was smelly – and they didn't know what was going to happen to them. One of the sixteen, a young woman called Isabella, decided that she could not just sit back and let herself be trapped there forever, or worse – killed and eaten! She knew she had to escape to get help and to save all of the other girls who were trapped in the cave before it was too late. Whilst the wyrm was sleeping she slowly crept towards the exit of the cave. To her dismay, she discovered that the wyrm had sneakily blocked the exit with a large rock! After frantically looking around for a way to move the rock she noticed a shaft of moonlight – there was a small opening at the top of the cave that she had not seen before because it was almost overgrown with bushes. She hitched up her gown and climbed to the very top of the cave, not looking down once, and managed to squeeze through the opening! As she clambered out she heard the wyrm starting to stir so she rushed to get away before he could notice that she had gone.

Isabella ran through the woods as fast as she could, stumbling over rocks, tripping over branches and wading through streams until she reached the first farm at the edge of the forest. She banged on the door of the farmhouse until someone answered. A farmer named William answered the door, along with his son Scaw. Isabella explained what had happened and that sixteen daughters from farms around Loftus, Handale and Liverton had been kidnapped by the dreadful, terrifying creature that had been stealing livestock from the farms for some time. William and Scaw jumped straight into action. William got on his horse and galloped to all of the local farms to raise the alarm. Scaw, a strong and bright young man, was an apprentice at a blacksmiths and had been working on a project to create his own type of armour. This armour was made of leather, to keep it flexible, but soaked in alum, making it extra strong and fire resistant. He pulled it out from the secret

DE DRACONE.

box underneath his bed and climbed into it, then reached under the bed again and pulled out his grandfather's old Crusader sword which he kept clean and sharp – just in case it was needed. Then he and Isabella set out to return to the wyrm's lair.

Isabella and Scaw ran swiftly through the woods, back the way she had come, and whilst they ran they decided what they would do. It was dawn by the time they reached the cave and Isabella clambered back on top of the cave so that she could drop down when the time was right. Scaw struck a large rock with his sword to attract the attention of the wyrm. Sure enough, the rock covering the cave moved to the side and out came the snake, hissing and breathing fire. Scaw put the visor down on his helmet and lunged for the beast, ready for a fight. He darted in and out between rocks as quickly as a cat, avoiding the flames and the poisonous sting at the end of the wyrm's tail. He was fearless and fought with bravery, no matter how the snake attacked him.

Whilst this was happening Isabella had dropped back into the cave and was getting all of the other girls out and to safety. One by one, they ran from the cave with instructions from Isabella to get to the edge of the woods as quickly as possible where they would be safe and reunited with their families. As the last maiden left the cave Isabella watched as Scaw continued his battle with the serpent. She noticed that he was not moving as quickly and was starting to tire. She racked her brains to decide what to do, but then an idea came to her. It was risky, but Scaw had risked his life to save hers so why should she not do the same for him. Isabella filled her pockets with stones, then climbed a tree and drew attention to herself by throwing the stones at the wyrm and shouting as she did so. It was just enough to distract the snake from the fight. As the wyrm drew itself to its full height, blew fire and lunged at Isabella, Scaw seized this opportunity, leapt through the air and sliced off the serpent's head with his sword. The battle was done.

Isabella and Scaw climbed over the body of the snake and headed back towards the edge of the woods. When they reached the farmhouse, all of the local farmers and their families were there crying and hugging their daughters who they had feared they would never see again. The Lord of the Manor, Ambrose Beckwith, was also there as his daughter Emma was best friends with the courageous Isabella. He rewarded Scaw with a large sum of money, and a small woodland to thank him for saving them all. Scaw then told Ambrose that he and Emma would like to be married, and her father agreed.

The people of Handale, Liverton and Loftus were never threatened by such a creature again and they knew that they were safe thanks to Scaw and to Isabella. Scaw and Emma had a very happy life together, and if you go to Handale Abbey farmhouse there is a stone coffin with a sword carved onto it – and some people say that there was a sword inside it and the words 'snake slayer' carved into the lid, but that this has been eroded away. Scaw Wood is still part of Handale Woods.

And what happened to Isabella? She certainly didn't go back to just being the daughter of a farmer. Although she had been scared, she had resourcefully overcome the ordeal and now had a taste for adventure. I wonder what she did next…?

RETOLD BY HELEN ATKINSON

The Man from Upsall

✦ A man from Upsall once journeyed to London. As he was standing on London Bridge, a Quaker approached and asked him what he was doing there. The Yorkshireman answered that on three consecutive nights he had dreamt that if he stood on London Bridge long enough he would hear something to his advantage. The Quaker seemed amused. He said he'd had a similar dream, that if he went to a place called Upsall and dug under an Elder bush in the grounds of a castle he would find a pot of gold. But he hadn't met anyone who'd ever heard of Upsall. The Upsall man kept quiet and hurried home, and, so the story goes, dug up a pot of gold.

A Guisborough Legend

✦ An underground passage running from twelfth-century Guisborough Priory to a field in Tocketts parish to the north of the town is reputed to hold a chest of gold guarded by a raven or crow. When an explorer tried to find the treasure, half-way along the passage he was confronted by a bird which transformed itself into the Devil and he fled in terror.

The Hermit of Falling Foss

A short walk from Falling Foss waterfall,[1] on the wooded footpath towards Littlebeck, is a cave carved out of a huge boulder.[2] Known as 'The Hermitage', it is thought that a sailor named Jeffery was responsible for the arduous task of carving out the interior room (which can seat twenty people) on the instructions of George Chubb, the local schoolmaster.[3] Inscribed above the door are the letters 'GC' and the date 1790, presumably the date the interior was created. There is a local tradition that a hermit once lived in the cave.

---

1 Accessible from the Forestry England car park at May Beck, 6 miles south of Whitby, at NZ 892 024.
2 NZ 885 040
3 www.fabulousfollies.net/eskdaleside.htmlnpress.lib.uiowa.edu/feminae

---

Nunnington Church Tomb

The effigy of Sir Walter de Teyes, who died in 1325, can be seen in the Church of All Saints and St James at Nunnington. Local legend, however, claims that this is the burial place of Peter Loschy, said to have been killed by a dragon in nearby Loschy Wood. The dragon was defeated by Loschy with the help of Loschy's dog, who carried pieces of dragon hacked off by his master and buried them in the churchyard. Sadly, Loschy succumbed to poisoning from the dragon's blood. There is a retelling of the story on the next page.

The Story of the Nunnington Dragon

✦ Nobody went near the den in those days. The smell festered all summer, noxious fumes swirling down the valley.

When Peter Loschy passed through the village with his little dog, he held his nose.

'How can you bear the smell?' the young knight asked. 'It's… it's unpalatable.'

John the blacksmith shrugged. Most of the villagers looked away.

Peter tried to rouse them to a fury. 'Aren't you angry,' he asked, 'about what the beast has done to you?'

Too many villagers had been taken by then – too many to count. Yes, they were angry once. But Peter's question was returned by blank-eyed stares and dark eyes glassy like a frog's.

At last he said: 'I'll get him!' because it seemed the most obvious sort of thing to do.

Perhaps Peter expected praise or gratitude, but all he got in return was a tut or two and a shaking of heads.

'I will get him!' he said to John.

'Or he'll get you…'

There's a trick to defeating a dragon, be they serpents or worms, of the flying kind or squirming in the dirt. You just need to plan it all out.

'You stay here,' Peter told his dog. 'Keep safe.'

Then Peter fashioned for himself a very great suit – a very clever suit, or so he thought. John had told him that the beast's method of inflicting death was to coil around its prey and squeeze. Squeeze the living breath out of them.

Patiently, John helped Peter to bejewel his suit with a thousand spikes, razor-sharp. It shimmered as though it were a very special thing indeed.

When Peter approached the den, the sun danced upon his back and sword so that the serpent paused before it wound around him as it had done many times before. Slowly it coiled, slowly, round and up…

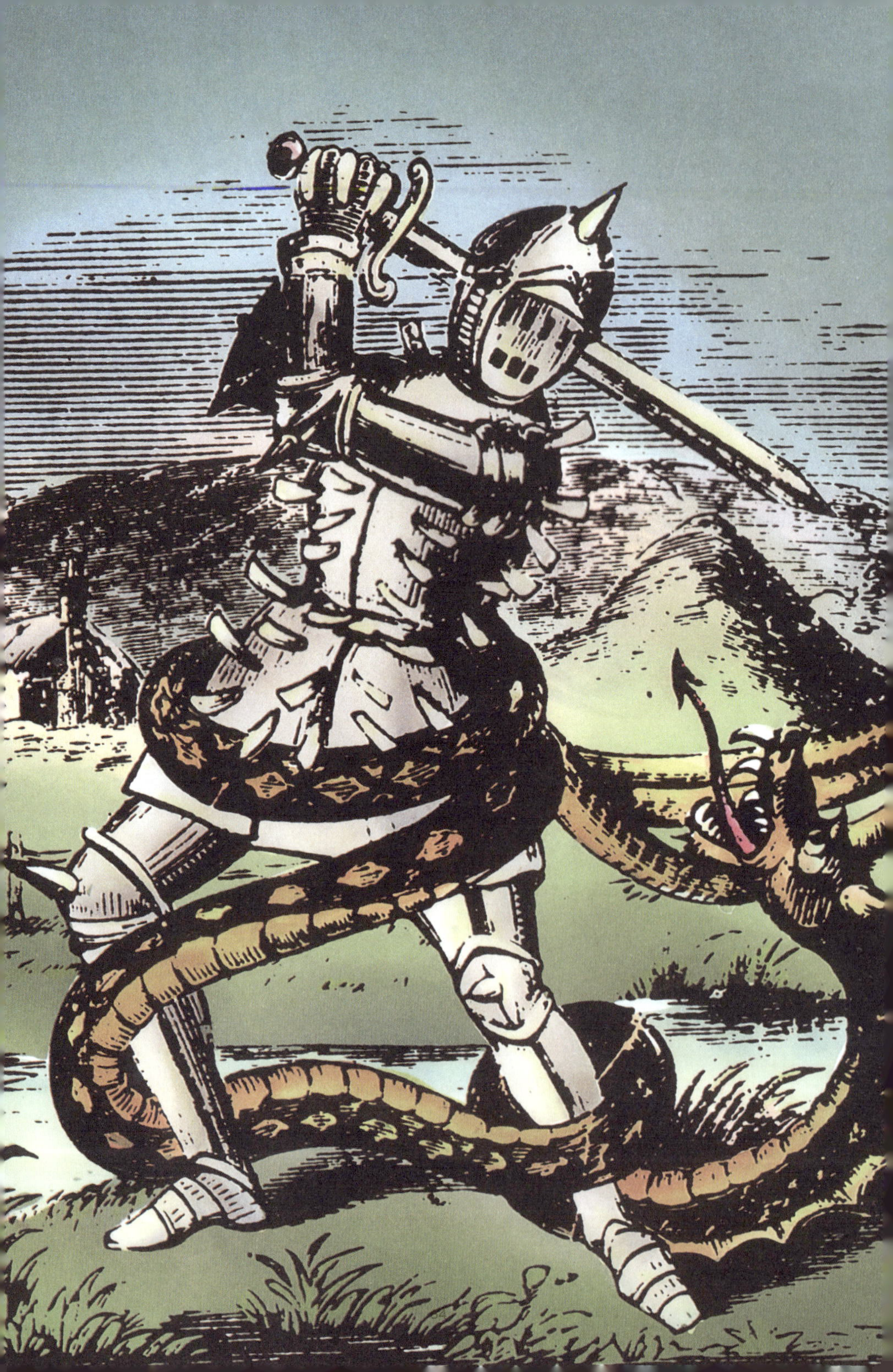

Then…

A squeal, which cut the air. The creature reared. His prey was free.

Dragon blood is very strange, the texture gloopy and unnatural, it seemed to Peter then. He felt his head turn dizzy at the sight and smell.

But the dragon did not fall, though he'd been deeply pierced by Peter's suit. Instead, it rose again. Peter watched, astonished, to see the ribboned flesh restore.

'How?' he gasped.

How, indeed, can a dragon heal? But Peter didn't have time for a question like that. The dragon rose and Peter raised his sword. But even the most deadly stab was healed at once.

All morning, Peter stabbed and speared. He pierced and wounded. But by afternoon, he was tiring. His breath came sharp and ragged then until he found himself cowering beneath a rock. He wouldn't last much longer.

But something nuzzled against Peter's hand, something soft and warm. His little dog.

'You were supposed to keep safe,' he whispered. 'No matter, I'm glad you came.'

Peter felt his spirits restored. Reaching forward, he hacked the serpent's tail. Thwack! And something changed.

The little dog seized the piece of dragon flesh and ran, and ran. He bounded over tufts and hedges. At the churchyard, he buried the tip of tail before returning to take a claw.

All day they fought like this. Peter hacked. The little dog carried. Smaller and smaller the dragon shrank, piece by piece until at last it was dispatched.

If you like happy endings, now is the time to stop. Let's leave them there, on that hillside, man and dog, companionable and still, to take a moment to enjoy their victory.

Let's not tell the end of the tale, of how the exhausted knight fell to rest, and how his faithful dog, his face smeared in poisoned blood, tried to revive him and with that friendly toxic lick sealed his young master's fate.

Let us leave them resting only, on Loschy Hill together.

RETOLD BY ROSIE BARRETT

Fairy Rings

Fairy stories are thought to have origins in ancient animistic beliefs. The old ideas that spirits inhabit natural objects (such as trees, rocks, waterfalls...) and cause natural phenomena are far removed from many people's world views today, but they still exist in popular tales handed down over generations and continue to enrich our imaginations.

If we were to draw a fairy we'd have plenty of cultural references. William Blake's depiction of Oberon (King of the Fairies), Titania and Puck from Shakespeare's play *Midsummer Night's Dream* is a famous example.[1] Painted in 1786, it features a group of fairies dancing in a circle, a typical activity of fairies according to folklore. Their delight and playfulness are plain to see.

Oberon, Titania and Puck with Fairies Dancing by William Blake (1786).

Early illustration of witches and devilish creatures dancing in a ring.

Seventeenth-century woodcut showing a fairy circle.

Much of our folklore comes from the Victorian era. Folklorist Wirt Sykes, writing in 1880, collected many accounts of fairies who were invariably described as dancing in a group when encountered.

It may come as a surprise to learn that the collected folklore often relates fairies with witches. Both were portrayed as mischievous, feared for their ability to curse people, and having supernatural powers that were frowned upon by the Church. Both were believed to dance in circles, usually on moonlit nights. The rings created by their dancing feet, known as 'fairy rings', or sometimes 'hag tracks',[2] only becoming visible to humans the following morning.[3]

Fairy rings appear as mysterious circles of darker grass, or in some cases dozens of mushrooms growing in a circle. Of the latter type, one Welsh woman claimed that the fairies used the mushrooms as parasols and umbrellas.[4]

Many folk stories and superstitions suggest that fairy rings are best avoided. This traditional Scottish rhyme sums up the dangers:

He wha tills the fairies' green
Nae luck again shall hae:
And he wha spills the fairies' ring
Betide him want and wae.
For weirdless days and weary nights
Are his till his deein' day.
But he wha gaes by the fairy ring,
Nae dule nor pine shall see,
And he wha cleans the fairy ring
An easy death shall dee.[5]

Entering a fairy ring on the European Christian feast day of Saint Walpurga ('May Eve') or the night of Halloween is especially perilous.[6] Some stories suggest that an enchanted victim may be plucked out by someone from the

| Plucked from the fairy circle – a man saves his friend from the grip of a fairy ring.[7]

outside, though a tale from a Welsh farmer who had to tie a rope around himself and enlist the help of four men to save his daughter, suggests this was by no means an easy feat. Other stories required simply casting wild marjoram and thyme into the circle to confuse the fairies.

FAIRY CROSS PLAIN

In the Esk Valley area of the North York Moors, Fairy Cross Plain has a long association with fairies and folklore. This central piece of rising ground between Little Fryup Dale and Great Fryup Dale has a distinctive grassy knoll, as can be seen to the right in the photograph above.[8]

Rev. J.C. Atkinson records a conversation in the 1860s with one of his parishioners which suggests the origin of the name 'Fairy Cross Plain':

'Just a little in front of where the public-house at the Plains now stands, in the old days, before the roads were made as they are now, two ways or roads used to cross, and that gave the "cross" part of the name. And as to the rest of it, or the name "Fairy", everybody knows that years and years ago the fairies had "a desper't haunt o' thae hill-ends just a-hint (behind) the Public." '[9]

The public house he was referring to was the Ship Inn.[10]

Peter Walker, born and bred in Glaisdale and a prolific author (under the pseudonym Nicholas Rhea), remembered playing at Fairy Cross Plain as a child. He recalled how local people would dance nine times around the grassy circles in the light of a full moon, quietly so they could listen for the mischievous laughter of the fairies in their fairy kingdom beneath their feet. But locals knew they should never dance round the rings more than nine times…[11]

As another parishioner from Rev. Atkinson's time explained:

'This would have given the fairies power over us, and they would have come and taken us away for good, to go and live where they lived… The mothers used to

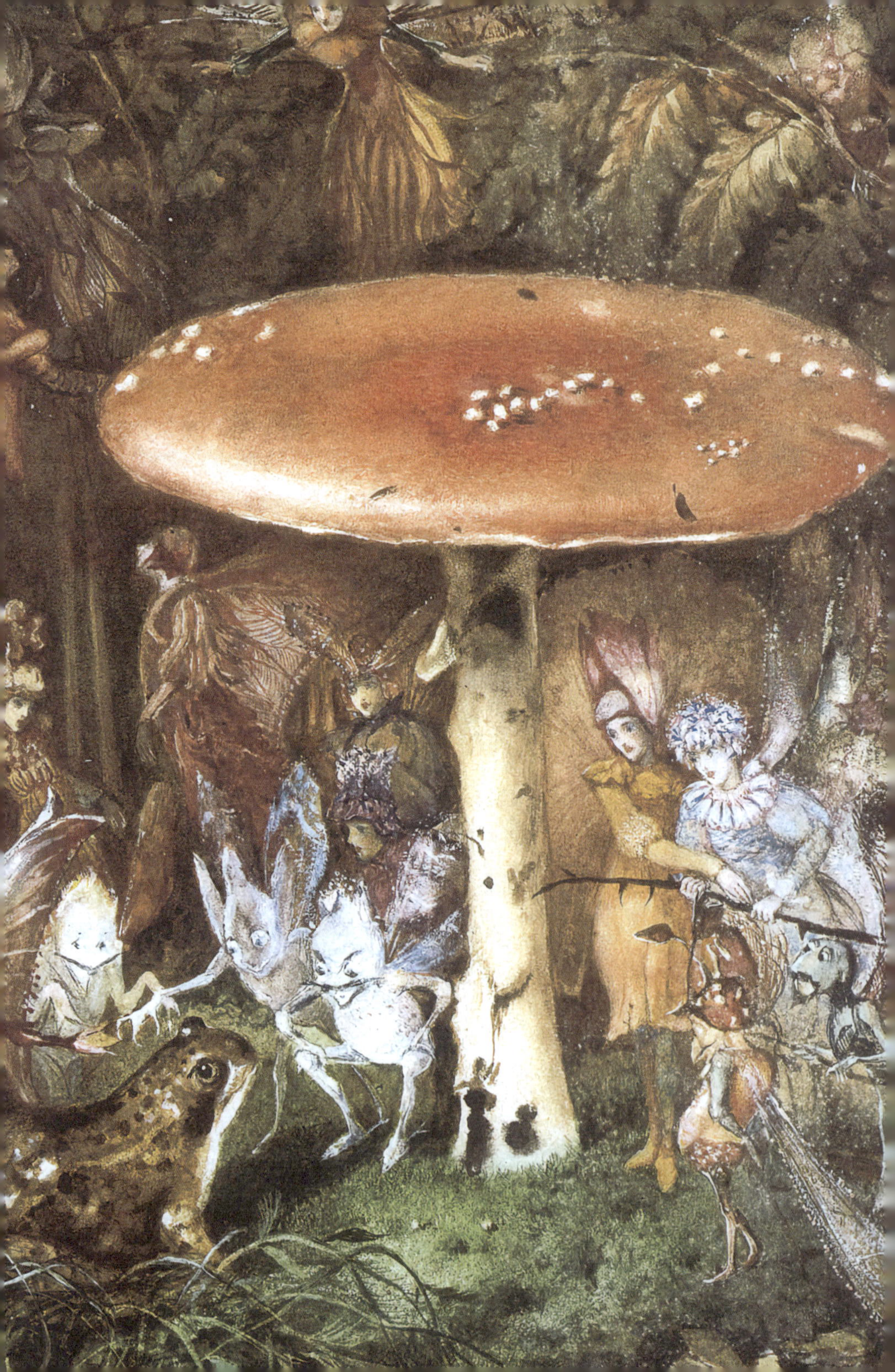

Fairy Ring Champignon (*marasmius oreades*) and its effect on grassland.

threaten us, if we weren't good, that they would turn us to the door (out of doors) at night, and then the fairies would get us.'

With scientific thinking came an understanding that fairy circles of the type seen in Fryupdale were in fact created by a fungus (*Fairy Ring Champignon – marasmius oreades*) which spreads across grassland creating circles in ever-expanding rings.

Science has given us an explanation for the so-called fairy rings of Fryup. The pub at Fairy Cross Plain has long gone – now a cluster of dwellings on the road near the Yorkshire Cycle Hub. The magical knoll has been planted with trees. Our world views have changed. And yet folktales and the name 'Fairy Cross Plain' on a map remain. And the fairies? Well, they're still there aren't they?

NICOLA CHALTON

Opposite: *The Intruder* (c. 1860) by John Anster Fitzgerald, with a fly agaric centre stage.

1   'Oberon, Titania and Puck with Fairies Dancing' by William Blake, c. 1786
2   Oxford English Dictionary's earliest evidence for hag track is from 1836, in the writing of William Durrant Cooper, antiquary
3   *The Fairy Mythology: Illustrative of the Romance and Superstition of Various Countries*, by T. Keightley, 1828
4   *Fairylore: Memorates and Legends from Welsh Oral Tradition*, R. Gwyndaf, 1991
5   *The Popular Rhymes of Scotland with illustrations, chiefly collected from oral sources*, R. Chambers, 1826
6   *The Encyclopedia of Superstitions*, E. Radford; M.A. Radford, 1946
7   *British Goblins: Welsh Folklore, Fairy Mythology, Legends and Traditions* by W. Sikes, 1880
8   Mick Garratt, 'Little Fryup Dale', 'Out & About on the North York Moors', www.fhithich.uk
9   *Forty Years in a Moorland Parish*, Rev J.C. Atkinson, 1891, page 51
10 Ordnance Survey Six-inch England and Wales, 1842–1952; via 'Out & About on the North York Moors', Little Fryup Dale, www.fhithich.uk
11 'Fryup – a dale of horses and fairy rings', Peter Walker (1936–2017), *Darlington & Stockton Times*, 2 May 2014

Antiquities of Goathland

Landmarks, traditions and folklore of the moorland village of Goathland are revealed in this 1910 lecture by Mr Oxley Graham, curator of the Yorkshire Philosophical Society's museum.

The name Goathland is said to derive either from 'Godeland', i.e. Godland, being an early settlement of Christians, or from 'Gothland', being an early settlement of Goths.

Hermitage of Goathland

The ecclesiastical establishment at Goathland was initially a hermitage, granted by Henry I, in 1117, to Osmund, a priest, and a few brethren who took up their habitation there as a place to distribute alms to the poor. The hermitage was dedicated to St Mary and probably stood about a mile north-east of the present chapel at Abbot's House, now in the possession of the Harwoods. Peter Harwood's obligation for holding his lands is that he keeps an entire house, a bull and a bear for the use of the parish and that he blows a horn from the top of Silhouse each morning at six o'clock.

John Hill, 'a man of many parts'

John Hill, formerly landlord of the Cross Pipes, closed in 1867, and now of the new Goathland Hotel, is described as 'a man of many parts': a sexton, bellringer and clerk of the local parish church, playing the small fiddle in church on Sundays. He also held the post of parish constable from 1864 to 1872, still having the old Goathland staff in his possession. Before harmoniums were used, the band in church on Sundays consisted of first and bass fiddles, clarinet and bassoon.

Goathland Church

In the old Goathland church[1] there used to be a grand font; for many years it was used as a pig trough and now it is in Grosmont church. The Goathland church chalice is unique. The bowl is shallow and conical and unlike any later examples. It might best be compared with the fourteenth-century chalices of York Minster and Hamstall Ridware. The general form of the chalice suggests an early date, certainly before 1450. After being sold, it was found in a shop in Carlisle and recovered.

Julian Park

Close to Goathland and on the opposite side of the beck is a farm known as July or Julian Park. The remains of the original park wall and its dyke can still be followed for a considerable distance in certain places, as can the foundations of an old castle, which might have been a Roman station to begin with. The local idea is that Julius Caesar kept his deer there, but Julius Caesar never got so far north as this. The place could have been named after Julius Briganticus, a Roman general mentioned by Tacitus in the reign of Vespasian AD 70, or perhaps was the retreat of a hermit called Julian.

In the year 1294 Lord Peter de Mauley sometimes resided at Mulgrave Castle and sometimes at July Park, at the castle called St Julian's. Lord Peter de Mauley was a native of Pointon in France; in the reign of Richard I he married Isabella, the only daughter of Robert Turnham, and obtained all her large estates, which included these two castles. She had inherited them from the Saxon Duke Wada, who in the year 800 lived at Mulgrave Castle and was a principal conspirator amongst those who murdered Ethelred, King of Northumberland.

Roman Road

The Roman road in the neighbourhood of Goathland is known as Wade Wife's Causey. According to local legends, Wade and his wife and son possessed the powers of the ancient Titans. Generally ascribed to their gigantic operations are the Roman road and the castles of Mulgrave and Pickering; the Roman road was to communicate between the two and to several Druidical stones in the neighbourhood. All trace of milestones on the Roman road have been lost, evidently broken up for use as gate posts and mending roads.

The moors around Goathland all abound in tumuli, stone cairns and cists. Most have been opened by Mr T. Kendall, Canon Greenwell and Canon Atkinson in days gone by and very many interesting relics by way of pottery, stone and metal implements of various kinds, weapons, ornaments etc, have been found.

Body Snatching

Close to Mauley Cross (on nearby Pickering Moors)[2] lives Willie Eddon, aged ninety-five, a wonderful old chap for his age. As a young man, in the days of the body snatchers, he'd earned a good bit of money taking corpses in his cart, acting as a carrier between Pickering and Beverley and Beverley and Hull. The corpses were put out ready for collection on churchyard walls and he carried them to the outskirts of Hull, where doctors and medical students, who needed them for anatomical studies, would relieve him of his ghastly burden. Body snatching had reached a high pitch in those days and men were stationed at churchyards with orders to shoot anyone entering during the hours of darkness; it would have been an awkward matter for old Willie if he had been caught, but he never was.

Nanny Pierson

The Goathland 'witch', Nanny Pierson, is said to have spent a week in Pickering in 1799 and to have announced on her return that it was a 'despert recklesome place and full of Satan and his carrying-ons'.

---

1 For more about the history of Goathland old church and the present one, built in 1892, see www.goathland.com
2 See 'Old Wives' Well' at www.fhithich.uk

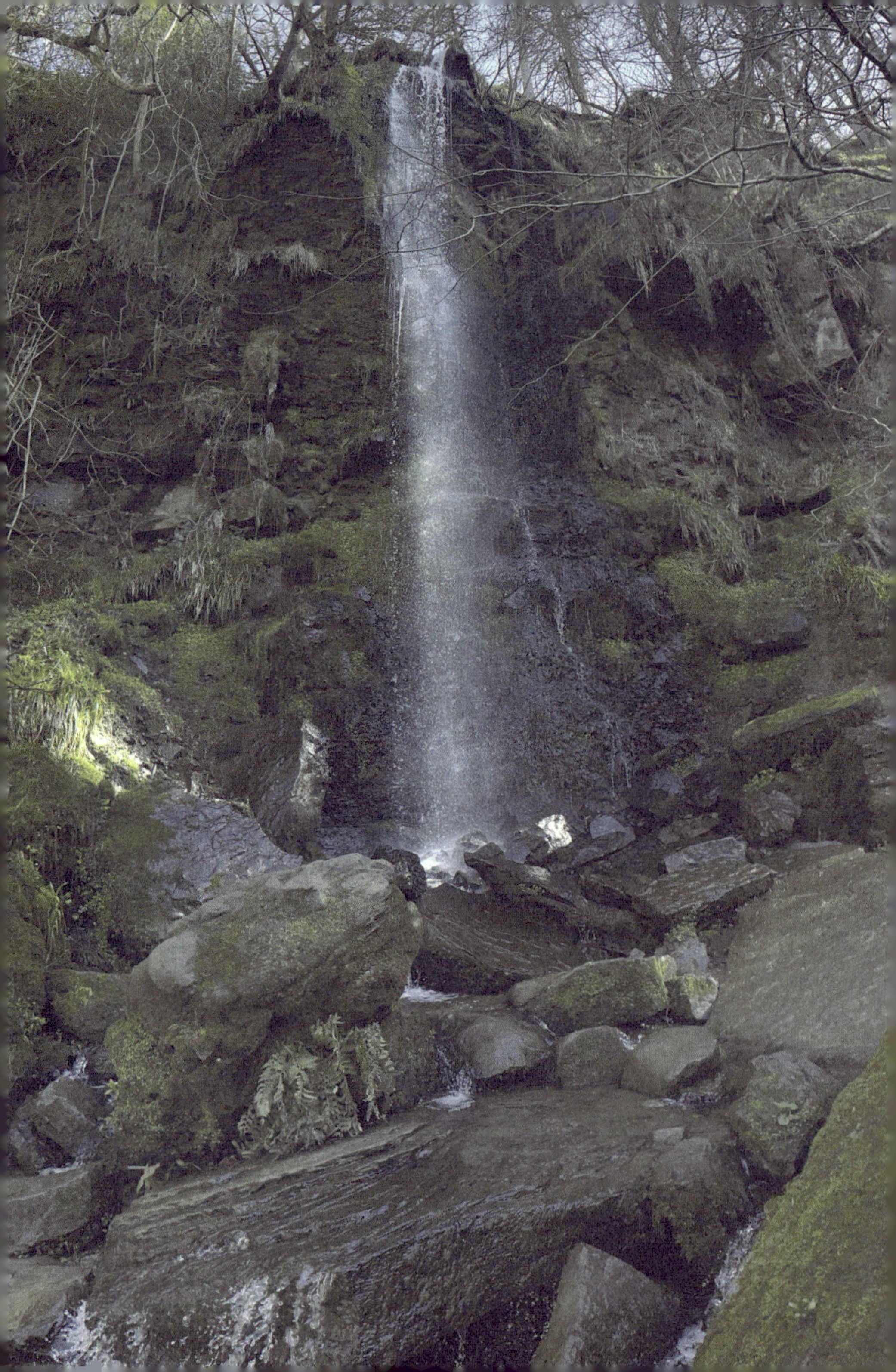

The Gytrash of Goathland

In the far off days when Arthur ruled in Camelot and the Kingdom of Northumbria stretched from the Humber to the Forth, the Vale of the Murk Esk[1] was held by Julian of Goathland from Allerston Moor. It was a wild and lonely land. Many a traveller had gone astray on those bewildering moors which ring it round and seem to have no end.

Here Julian minded to build himself a castle and for it he chose a spot which is known as Julian Park to this day. He could have made no better choice, for indeed it is a lovely place, hanging over the green woodlands which fringe the beck and hard by to Mallyan Spout, where the water throws itself over a cliff.

Little cared Julian for the beauty of the place. It was enough for him that here he could build a strong castle in which he could defy marauding neighbours and from which he could safely extract what he held to be his dues from the common folk on his lands. He was a hard and cruel man. He recked nought of the White Christ, but worshipped Woden and Thor, so far as he regarded any gods but his own fierce will, and it was a bitter lord to all who were beneath his power.

Now Julian of Goathland held by the old creed that if any house was to be securely built, life must be built in with it and since he was resolved that the new Castle Julian should be able to withstand the assaults of all his enemies and endure forever to the glory of his name, he swore a great oath by the Ravens of Woden that whosoever was the best beloved of the maidens of Eskdale should be walled up in the foundations of his keep and there be left to perish miserably. Among them all was found one so much beloved or so fair as Gytha, the only child of Gudrun of the Mill, and therefore as soon as the building began he sent his men at arms and took her from her father's house.

Gytha was at her spinning-wheel when they took her and they brought her before her lord with the spindle still in her hand. But when his purpose was known many of the people of Goathland followed after the men at arms and

Opposite: Mallyan Spout Waterfall, Goathland.

made their way into the presence of Julian to entreat him to spare the maid. But he only laughed at them and their tears and prayers and declared that he would give them a lesson in the obedience which his people owed to their lord. Wherefore he ordered his men at arms to seize Gudrun of the Mill, who had been loudest in his prayers for his daughter's life, and commanded that he himself should build the walls of his daughter's living tomb. When Gudrun refused, saying that he would rather die any death than to do this fearful thing, Julian tortured him with fire for many days until his spirit was altogether broken within him and he obeyed like a man in a dream.

But when there remained but two stones to be laid they placed by the side of the road a beaker of water and a loaf of bread – for Julian was angry with the murmuring of the people of Goathland and would not have had her die too soon – and in mockery of her wretchedness he added also her spindle and spinning wheel, saying that it was not well for maids to be idle and that perchance she might find the time hang heavy upon her hands. And so the wall of the foundation was finished and the wailing girl was shut away for ever from the light.

There was little strength in the law in Northumbria in those days and though many came and told the King of this deed and entreated him to avenge it, and the priests of Christ who were newly come to the land but had gained great power with him, he feared to move against Julian lest he should ally himself with the many and powerful enemies of the kingdom. So nothing was done against him, and when the Hermit of Eskdaleside visited Julian to bid him to repent, he laughed and set his great dogs on him so that the holy man barely escaped with his life.

The next year on the night of the day on which the maiden had been sacrificed, Julian was lying on his bed planning to add this and that to the castle he was building, when he and all within the house heard the wail of a woman coming, as it seemed, from the foundations of the keep. The wailing sound came nearer and nearer to the room in which he lay and when he would have called his guards he found that his tongue refused its office, nor could he himself move hand or foot. Presently the door of his chamber opened, and he was aware of a white figure clothed in what seemed to be the garments in which Gytha had worn when she was entombed, and bearing a spindle in her hand.

The figure spoke no word, but came and stood at the foot of his bed, still wailing, and he knew it was the wraith of the murdered Gytha come to extract vengeance, which neither the King's councillors nor the priests had been able to win. For some moments she stood motionless, and then very slowly she stretched out her right arm and held the spindle over his feet.

Criss-cross, criss-cross, criss-cross, three times she moved the spindle over the foot of the bed, and as she moved it, it seemed as though invisible threads were being wound about his feet and ankles, threads which no power of his could break. Then, still gently wailing, she turned and left him and it seemed to him, as the sound grew more distant, that she was returning to her grave in the keep. Upon him there came a great horror, but not until the wailing had altogether died away was he able to cry out or to rise, but at last power returned to him and he struggled from his bed.

But when he stood up his feet felt strangely numb and he could only shuffle along with a queer tottering gait. Neither the next day, nor the next, or any day, did the life come back to those dead feet of his. For a year he must go shuffling on dead feet, growing, as it seemed, neither worse nor better, until the fatal night came round once more. Then again the wailing of the Spinning Maiden was heard, and again he saw her figure with the spindle in her hand. But this time she waved it criss-cross, criss-cross, criss-cross above his knees and again he seemed to be bound with the same invisible threads.

The next day and for all that year he was dead from the knees downwards, only in that year strange and cruel pains that came and went as suddenly as the lightening shot through his body from time to time and in his agony he would cry out and curse his gods. He sent for the old Hermit of Eskdaleside and offered to turn Christian and build him a church if he would but pray to the God of the Christians to heal him and deliver him from his great distress.

The Hermit took his confession and set about building a church where Goathland Church now stands, but there was no remedy. Each year on the appointed night the Spinning Maiden came again with her dreadful spindle and each time she wound the invisible threads a little higher than the last. For ten years the Lord of Castle Julian died slowly from the feet upwards and always he suffered intolerable pains until at last his soul passed from him during the night of a great storm.

Now here the tale becomes broken and confused and it is not easy to say why the Gytrash came at this time, but some will have it that the Gytrash was the wraith of Julian himself, doomed to wander on earth and do yet more evil than he had done in his life.

All that is certainly known is that one of the men of Goathland was making his way home through the storm and when he was passing the church a gigantic black goat, with eyes that burned like live coals and horns tipped with fire, sprang over the churchyard wall and rushed past him. According to the account the man gave of it when he reached his home, the apparition made no sound either when it leaped the wall of the churchyard or when it dashed close past him, but he particularly noticed that when it rushed away along the road, he could hear the sound of its footfalls, a sound not at all like the clattering of a goat's hooves over hard ground, but a soft padding noise like that made of a man running with bare feet.

This at least was all that the neighbours could make of the story he told, for he reached his home in such a state of terror as to be almost incoherent. Nor was there at that time any means of testing his tale of 'Padfoot', as the villagers named the creature, for the man never recovered from his fright, but sickened of some mysterious malady which affected his mind as well as his body, and of which in due course he died.

However the people soon had plenty of opportunities of confirming the truth of the dead man's story, for the appearances of the Gytrash became so frequent that the whole countryside was thrown into panic. Men coming home in the evening after their work would hear the pad, pad, pad of the monstrous goat and run as they might, the horrible thing always overtook them before they could gain the shelter of their homes. It never touched any of them, but whosoever was overtaken by the goat most surely sickened the next day of the mysterious malady and was marked for death. During these sad days it is said that a blood-curdling shriek was heard from time to time across the moors, which the people attributed to the Gytrash.

Be that as it may, the Gytrash was by no means the only terror with which they had to contend, for the spirit of the Spinning Maiden was still unlaid. At midnight on every anniversary of her death the same wailing sound was heard to come from the keep of the castle and that year whoever was fairest and most beloved of the maids of the countryside was sure to die.

Engraving by Francis Holl, 1800-1899 (Wellcome Library).

Very naturally the people turned first of all to the Church for help and begged the Hermit of Eskdaleside to come to their assistance, but his interference proved quite ineffectual.

The distressed people were then determined to call in magical help and sent a deputation to the Spaewife of Fylingdales, who was considered to be the most competent witch in those parts, able to change herself into a hare when she was summoned to the Witches' Sabbaths on Whorle Hill and desired to elude observation. The Spaewife gave the deputation a more civil reception than they had any right to expect, considering the treatment she usually met with. She told them to come again that day week, when she hoped to have found out some remedy for their troubles.

What magic she practised in the interval remained her secret, but when they returned at the appointed time she told them that deliverance was to be found in a proper interpretation of the words 'Tane to tither'. She was forbidden to tell them what that was – they must make it out for themselves and she added that they had best set their wits to work, for, if they failed to discover it, the wraith of the Spinning Maiden would never be laid and the Gytrash would continue his marauding until the whole countryside was made desolate.

'Tane to Tither'. The words seemed to have no bearing upon the case and for weeks the elders of the village debated the question at their evening's meetings in the ale-house, without coming to any conclusion. At last it occurred to one intelligent fellow that the meaning of the Speawife's words must be that they should somehow set one of the phantoms to deal with the other, and that perhaps the magic threads of the Maiden would suffice to bind the Gytrash and so to rid them of their worst trouble. If there was anything in the idea, the Gytrash must somehow be decoyed into some kind of prison and the Maiden be persuaded to weave her threads round it so as to keep him fast.

Now it is well known that these Gytrashes have a particular liking for newly buried corpses, from which it is supposed that they draw their life, and it had been noticed that the Goathland Gytrash invariably hunted the neighbourhood of any newly made grave for some nights after the dead had been laid to rest. The village elders determined therefore to wait for the night on which the Spinning Maiden was abroad and then to lure the Gytrash by a mock funeral into the place where they intended to prepare for him. And so they dug the Killing Pit.

To discover how to persuade the Maiden to do her part when the Gytrash had been decoyed into the chosen pit, the elders again had recourse to the Speawife of Fylingdales. She congratulated and told them that they need have no fear of the Maiden giving them her help, for she said it had been revealed to her that between the Maiden and the Gytrash there existed a mortal enmity. All that was required was that they should lay a trail of honey from the castle to the pit and sprinkle it with corn and salt. That would suffice to guide the Maiden to the appointed spot and the rest they could safely leave to the phantom herself.

Then the people of Goathland made a Mell Baby out of a corn sheaf, as the folk of that part were wont to do when the last of the harvest was carried, and got it ready with great secrecy for that fateful night. They dressed the Baby in corpse clothes and put it in a coffin, mourning the while as though for some dead friend. Next, having laid the trail of honey, corn and salt, the mourners, weeping and bewailing themselves, bore the coffin through the village and laid it in the Killing Pit a little before midnight.

At midnight the padding of the Goat's footsteps was heard near at hand and in another moment the dreadful creature himself appeared, his eyes blazing like hot coals and his great horns tipped with fire. He disappeared in the pit and at the same moment the figure of the Spinning Maiden with the spindle in her hand was seen approaching along the track. It was noticed that on her calm face was the look of one who sees a great deliverance at hand.

When she reached the pit she stretched her hand over it and began to weave with her spindle criss-cross, criss-cross, criss-cross, weaving her thread over the Goat as she had woven it over Julian of Goathland. And the magic thread held true. From the bottom of the pit came a horrible cry such as that which the villagers had heard from time to time coming across the moors, but of the Gytrash himself nothing was seen. As the Maiden wove with her spindle the sides of the pit fell in until at last all was filled up as though no pit had been dug in that place. Yet still today there is one spot near the Killing Pit on which the grass never grows.

When the Maiden's task was accomplished a gentle smile was seen upon her sad face. Slowly, very slowly, she raised her arms above her head, dropping the spindle as she did so, and then she faded away in the moonlight and neither she nor the Gytrash troubled the people of Goathland again.

Abridged from *The Gytrash of Goathland and Other Yorkshire Legends* by Michael Temple, 1928.

---

[1] 'Mirk', meaning dark in colour, is probably the meaning associated with the Murk Esk, a tributary of the Esk. Ref: https://yorkshiredictionary.york.ac.uk/words/mirk

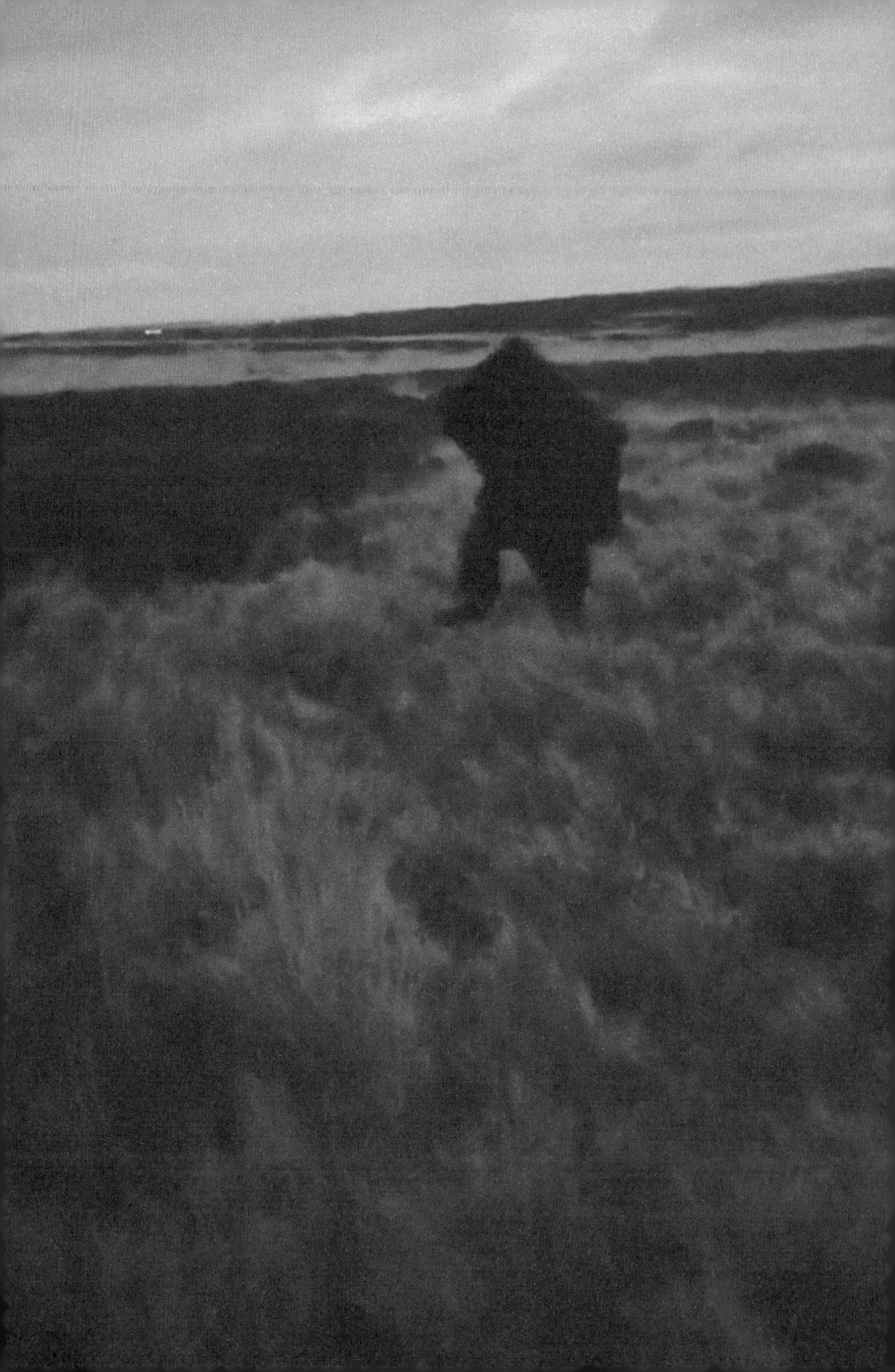

The Mysterious Beast of the Moors

There are numerous legends of a beast haunting the local moorland, the best known of which being that of the 'Barguest', dating back as far as the fourteenth century. Peter Walker, in his book *Folk Tales from the North York Moors*,[1] gives the following account:

'A barguest was a fearsome apparition which appeared shortly before the death of a local person. (…) There are barguests which have the form of huge animals, such as: black dogs, white cats, calves, pigs, goats, large rabbits, and other evil creatures which took the form of domestic animals. Whatever their appearance, they were never mistaken for ordinary domestic beasts because they had huge, saucer-like eyes, and feet which left no mark in the earth. (…) They supposedly issue terrifying roars or shrieks.'

A sighting was reported in the 1950s by Church of England Clergyman and notable exorcist, the Reverend Dr Donald Omand, after receiving a letter from a schoolmaster outlining his experience with such an apparition:

'On visiting Kettleness they [the schoolmaster and two friends] all experienced a wave of terror when, looking over the shore to the misty sea, they had seen a huge hound – so large it could not be mortal – appear out of thin air. Silent with shock

The ghostly Barguest, wood engraving, 1577.

The Black Dog features heavily in British folklore.

they watched it move towards them before disappearing as silently and mysteriously as it had come. All three were left with such a strong sense of evil that the schoolmaster believed it was a case desperately in need of exorcism.'[2]

Very recently, another sighting was reported. Mr Brocklehurst, a resident of the area, had the following words to describe his encounter:

'On the evening of 20 December 2023, I was driving through the moors of Danby in North Yorkshire and spotted a mysterious black figure in the shrubbery. Upon closer inspection, I found that it was some kind of very large cat-like creature, with a tail. There have long been local rumours and legends of a giant beast spotted in the moors called the Beast of Danby, matching this creature's description. I learned about it in school and the first sightings date back many decades. I believe I have got the very first video evidence of the Beast. I was very frightened but was able to film all of this until the creature got a little too close for comfort and I stopped filming and drove away.'[3]

No doubt keen researchers and investigators will now make a point of visiting the area and trying to solve the mystery. Have the North York Moors found their own Loch Ness Monster?

PASCAL THIVILLON

---

1   *Folk Tales from the North York Moors*, Peter N. Walker, Robert Hale, London, 1990
2   'To anger the Devil: Exorcist extraordinary The Reverend Dr Donald Omand', by M. Alexander, published by Neville Spearman Ltd, Suffolk, 1978
3   See the full video at: t.ly/y_vt1

Bell and Wade: A Tale of Two Giants

The Hole of Horcum

Long, long ago, before the appearance of human beings, it is said that giants roamed the earth. Two of them, Bell and her husband Wade, lived in the Whitby area. They were a busy couple, working hard everyday building various features that define the local landscape of today.

Bell kept a large cow across the moor. An enormous jawbone of a whale kept at Mulgrave Castle was once believed to be the rib of Bell's cow. The daily journey to go and milk the animal proved difficult at times in the boggy peat terrain. The two giants thus decided to built a stone road to make travelling easier. It is still to this day know as 'Wade's Causeway' or 'Wade's Wife Causey' and extends to the north and south of Wheeldale for up to 25 miles.[1]

During construction, Bell would bring along the stones for Wade to lay, carrying them in her apron. A few times, the weight of the stones proved too heavy for the fabric, and the stones were left behind as big piles of boulders that can still be found scattered around the moorland.

Laying roads wasn't their sole endeavour. They also had a thing for building castles! Strong and fierce as they were, they decided to build not one, but two of them simultaneously: one each. Wade was in charge of the construction of Mulgrave Castle, while Bell went about erecting Pickering Castle. A slight inconvenience: they only had one hammer to accomplish their task. But they wouldn't be stopped so easily. The solution was simple enough: with a shout of warning to avoid an accident, they threw the tool to each other across the moor when needed.

So went the daily life of our couple. But all wasn't always perfect in the couple's relationship. One time, Bell and Wade had a heated argument about some matter or other. Furious at his wife, Wade scooped a handful of earth, threw it angrily at Bell... and missed! That is how the Hole of Horcum and Blakey Topping were formed.

The couple carried on with their lives for many more years. Today, their legacy is visible in the local landscape, including a six-foot-high standing stone near East Barnby marking the head of Wade's grave, with a similar stone twenty yards apart marking the foot of the grave. It is not known where Bell is resting.

PASCAL THIVILLON

---

1 Nowadays a one-mile stretch of Wade's Causeway can be seen on Wheeldale Moor. In 1964 Hayes and Rutter concluded this was a Roman road due to the raised and cambered enbankment and other features.

Creatures Beneath the Waves

The idea of creatures beneath the waves, possessed of human form with fish-like extremities, has been around since antiquity. Roman author Pliny recorded that mermaids came on board ships at night, and plentiful tales spread all over the world of sailors' lives lost, lured by creatures with torsos of women and the scaly tails of large fish.

Mermaids of Staithes

A local legend from North Yorkshire's coast features the village of Staithes (locally known as 'Steears'), between Whitby and Saltburn. In Old English 'Staithes' means 'landing place'. This is where fishermen from earliest times landed their catch in a natural harbour between the two headlands of Cowbar Nab and Penny Nab.

During one terrible storm, two beautiful mermaids were washed ashore in the little harbour of Staithes. The villagers found the mermaids asleep and were filled with fear so locked them away where they could do no harm. Many came to gaze at the imprisoned creatures, some cruelly taunting them, even hitting them with sticks.

Over time the villagers became accustomed to the mermaids and stopped to talk to them, even trusting their release for certain village events. At one such event held on the beach, the mermaids saw their chance and escaped into the sea, but not before venting their fury by laying a curse on the village. 'The sea shall flow to Jackdaw's Well' they called as they left. This old well where flocks of jackdaws gathered was near Seaton Garth and the villagers laughed at the curse saying that the sea would never reach so far inland. But during the many years after this event, the cliffside around Staithes eroded, taking houses and fields into the sea, a storm claimed the lives of thirteen sailors, and Jackdaw's Well has long since disappeared.

Rituals and Superstitions

Fishing communities have always been vulnerable to loss of life from the furies of the sea. When boats left the relative safety of harbour, any number of things could go wrong. Rituals we now describe as superstitions were intended to protect the community from danger. Here are some examples from Staithes[1]:

It is of frequent occurrence that after having caught nothing for many nights, the fishermen will keep the first fish that comes into the boat and burn it on their return home as a sacrifice to the Fates.

All four-footed animals are considered unlucky, but the most ill omened of quadrupeds is the pig. If, when the men are putting their nets into the boats, the name of this innocent and succulent animal is by accident mentioned, they will always desist from their task and turn to some other occupation, hoping thus to avert the evil omen, and in many cases will renounce the day's expedition altogether, convinced that no good could come of it.

The sight of a drowned dog or kitten as a fisherman goes towards his coble[2] will always keep a Staithes fisherman at home.

As a fisherman walks to his boat, with lines on his head or a bundle of nets on his shoulder, and he chances to meet face to face with a woman, be she even his own wife or daughter, he will consider himself doomed to ill-luck. Thus, when a woman sees a man approaching her under these circumstances she at once turns her back on him.

If a fisher sends his son to fetch his big sea-boots, the bearer must be careful to carry them under his arm. Should he by inadvertence place them on his shoulder his father will inevitably refuse to put out to sea that day.

An egg is deemed so unlucky that the fishermen will not even use the word, but call the produce of a fowl a 'round-about'.

Fearless as are the fishers in their daily juggling with the dangers of the sea, yet so fearful are they of nameless spirits and bogies, that in the whole fishing colony of Staithes it would be impossible to find a volunteer who, for a couple of sovereigns, would walk by night to the neighbouring village of Hinderwell, a couple of miles distant.

Sea-Man of Skinningrove

Not far from Staithes, at the coastal village of Skinningrove, a sea-man, or merman, is recorded in the 1500s to have been caught in the nets of fishermen.[3] Here is a re-telling of the tale:

Usually, the men celebrated when the nets bulged under the weight of a catch.

But this catch was different. When pressed, some of them owned to feeling astonishment, perhaps, but kept their fear as quiet as their delight.

It's not every day that a sea-man is hauled ashore.

They kept him in an abandoned house and gave him raw fish to eat as all other food he refused. He responded to their prying eyes with remarkable patience, all things considered. Sometimes, they let the womenfolk enter his rooms and he gazed, transfixed, as though he were encountering something very new and wondrous. But he never spoke. Some say he only shrieked in a language none could discern.

One day, he stole away.

Some say they saw him return to sea. They say he looked back to the shore where he'd been kept these many weeks and something about the look of him gave the watchers the impression that he had enjoyed his time amongst them. That's what they say.

---

1 From *County Folk-Lore, Vol. II, Examples of Printed Folk-Lore Concerning the North Riding of Yorkshire, York and the Ainsty*, collected by Mrs Gutch, published for The Folk-Lore Society by David Nutt, 1901
2 Flat-bottomed fishing boat
3 Mention of the sea-man is found in the Cotton manuscripts (Julius F VI 1529-1610) held at the British Library

They Have a Legend Here That When a Ship is Lost Bells are Heard out at Sea...

Mina Murray is the main female character in Bram Stoker's 1897 novel *Dracula*. She is engaged to Jonathan Harker, an English solicitor. While Jonathan travels to Transylvania to act as an estate agent for a foreign client named Count Dracula who wishes to move to London, Mina is visiting her best friend Lucy Westenra - who will later become Count Dracula's first English victim - in Whitby. In her journal, Mina writes about her impressions of the town...

4 JULY - WHITBY

Lucy met me at the station, looking sweeter and lovelier than ever, and we drove up to the house at the Crescent in which they have rooms. This is a lovely place. The little river, the Esk, runs through a deep valley, which broadens out as it comes near the harbour. A great viaduct runs across, with high piers, through which the view seems somehow further away than it really is. The valley is beautifully green, and it is so steep that when you are on the high land on either side you look right across it, unless you are near enough to see down. The houses of the old town – the side away from us – are all red-roofed, and seem piled up one over the other anyhow, like the pictures we see of Nuremberg. Right over the town is the ruin of Whitby Abbey, which was sacked by the Danes, and which is the scene of part of 'Marmion', where the girl was built up in the wall. It is a most noble ruin, of immense size, and full of beautiful and romantic bits; there is a legend that a white lady is seen in one of the windows. Between it and the town there is another church, the parish one, round which is a big graveyard, all full of tombstones. This is to my mind the nicest spot in Whitby, for it lies right over the town, and has a full view of the harbour and all up the bay to where the headland called Kettleness stretches out into the sea. It descends so steeply over the harbour that part of the bank has fallen away, and some of the graves have been destroyed. In one place part of the stonework of the graves

'Right over the town is the ruin of Whitby Abbey'.

stretches out over the sandy pathway far below. There are walks, with seats beside them, through the churchyard; and people go and sit there all day long looking at the beautiful view and enjoying the breeze. I shall come and sit here very often myself and work. Indeed, I am writing now, with my book on my knee, and listening to the talk of three old men who are sitting beside me. They seem to do nothing all day but sit up here and talk.

The harbour lies below me, with, on the far side, one long granite wall stretching out into the sea, with a curve outwards at the end of it, in the middle of which is a lighthouse. A heavy sea-wall runs along outside of it. On the near side, the sea-wall makes an elbow crooked inversely, and its end too has a lighthouse. Between the two piers there is a narrow opening into the harbour, which then suddenly widens.

It is nice at high water; but when the tide is out it shoals away to nothing, and there is merely the stream of the Esk, running between banks of sand, with rocks here and there. Outside the harbour on this side there rises for about half a mile a great reef, the sharp edge of which runs straight out from behind the south lighthouse. At the end of it is a buoy with a bell, which swings in bad weather, and sends in a mournful sound on the wind. They have a legend here that when a ship is lost bells are heard out at sea. I must ask the old man about this; he is coming this way....

He is a funny old man. He must be awfully old, for his face is all gnarled and twisted like the bark of a tree. He tells me that he is nearly a hundred, and that he was a sailor in the Greenland fishing fleet when Waterloo was fought. He is, I am afraid, a very sceptical person, for when I asked him about the bells at sea and the White Lady at the abbey he said very brusquely:

'I wouldn't fash masel' about them, miss. Them things be all wore out. Mind, I don't say that they never was, but I do say that they wasn't in my time. They be all very well for comers and trippers, an' the like, but not for a nice young lady like you. Them feet-folks from York and Leeds that be always eatin' cured herrin's an' drinkin' tea an' lookin' out to buy cheap jet would creed aught. I wonder masel' who'd be bothered tellin' lies to them – even the newspapers, which is full of fool-talk.' I thought he would be a good person to learn interesting things from, so I asked him if he would mind telling me something about the whale-fishing in the old days. He was just settling himself to begin when the clock struck six, whereupon he laboured to get up, and said:

| 'This is to my mind the nicest spot in Whitby'.

'I must gang ageeanwards home now, miss. My grand-daughter doesn't like to be kept waitin' when the tea is ready, for it takes me time to crammle aboon the grees, for there be a many of 'em; an', miss, I lack belly-timber sairly by the clock.'

He hobbled away, and I could see him hurrying, as well as he could, down the steps. The steps are a great feature of the place. They lead from the town up to the church, there are hundreds of them – I do not know how many – and they wind up in a delicate curve; the slope is so gentle that a horse could easily walk up and down them. I think they must originally have had something to do with the abbey. I shall go home too. Lucy went out visiting with her mother, and as they were only duty calls, I did not go. They will be home by this.

• • •

1 AUGUST

I came up here alone, for I am very sad. There was no letter for me. I hope there cannot be anything the matter with Jonathan. The clock has just struck nine. I see the lights scattered all over the town, sometimes in rows where the streets are, and sometimes singly; they run right up the Esk and die away in the curve of the valley. To my left the view is cut off by a black line of roof of the old house next to the abbey. The sheep and lambs are bleating in the fields away behind me, and there is a clatter of a donkey's hoofs up the paved road below. The band on the pier is playing a harsh waltz in good time, and further along the quay there is a Salvation Army meeting in a back street. Neither of the bands hears the other, but up here I hear and see them both. I wonder where Jonathan is and if he is thinking of me!

I wish he were here.

The Hand of Glory

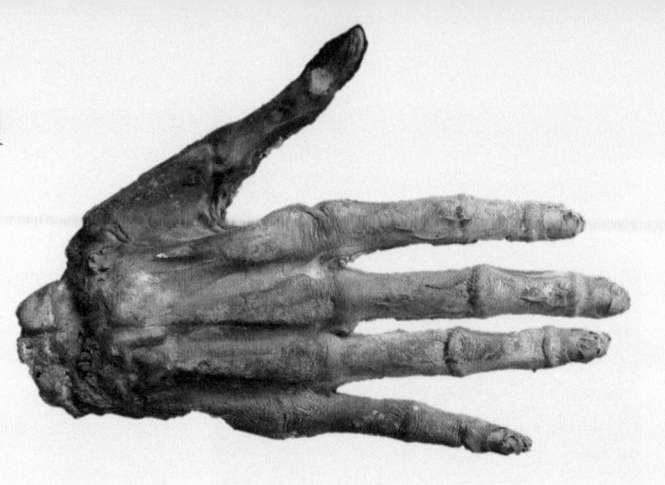

Whitby Museum houses a wide range of artefacts from around the Esk Valley, none more curious than the 'Hand of Glory'. This gory item, donated to Whitby Museum in 1935, was found by Dr J.E. Chalmers over the lintel of a house in Castleton he had recently purchased. The house was known to have previously been owned by a man of bad character, though nothing was ever proven. The hand was passed to Joseph Ford, a local mason with an interest in folklore who immediately recognised it as an example of a 'Hand of Glory'.

The name is thought to derive from the French 'main de gloire', a version of 'mandragore' or 'mandrake'. The mandrake, long regarded as having magical powers, was believed to grow beneath the gallows of a hanged man, with roots and leaves resembling hands.

Legend has it that a 'Hand of Glory' is the severed hand of a hanged felon, cut from the body while still hanging from the gibbet. Pickled for preservation, the hand was then used to either hold a candle or the fingers themselves were lit, sending any sleepers into a trance from which they could not be awakened until the light was extinguished. If the fingers were lit and the thumb refused to light it was a sign someone in the house was awake and could not be affected by the spell. This superstition made a 'Hand of Glory' a useful tool for burglars.

Legends from Northumberland to the North York Moors survive of the use of these gruesome objects. Most involve burglary though one relates to a young man stealing into his unwilling girlfriend's bed. The only preventative measure was to smear the threshold with an ointment of 'the gall of a black cat, the fat of a white hen and the blood of a screech owl'. The candle could only be extinguished using blood or skimmed milk to break the spell.

Let those who rest more deeply sleep;
Let those awake their vigils keep;
Oh, Hand of Glory, shed thy light;
Direct us to our spoil tonight.

The Whitby 'Hand of Glory' is the only alleged example known to exist.

SARAH PORTEUS

Gibbets and Gallows

GALLOW HOWE

'Have you ever stood in the dead hour of night on this moorland ridge and looked up into the heavens where the eternal stars are shining and where every point of light may be a world, or have you wondered and tried to guess what men and women may be doing up there? Will they be engaged in erecting gibbets on their moorland ridges…? Will the pale light of harvest moons shine down on them as they shine down on us, and will nocturnal birds witness such sights as they will have witnessed at Gallow Howe?'

Joseph Ford, in his book *Some Reminiscences and Folk Lore of Danby Parish and District*, was contemplating the events that led to the erection of an inscribed stone '**Gallow Howe**', dated 1835, on a stretch of moorland above Castleton village.

Ford describes how to reach the memorial:

'Walk along the road leading to Rosedale, a distance of some 420 yards, then turn to the right across the heather. Another 80 yards will bring you to the object of your search… The gibbet stood not far from the crossroads, which in those days led to Whitby, Stokesley and Kirkbymoorside.'

© Mick Garratt

He goes on to re-imagine some of the dramatic and painful scenes associated with the gibbet and how this place was once a source for the dreaded 'Hand of Glory':

'Atavistic instincts brought some poor wretch across these moorland tracks to this place of execution: more than one poor mother's heart in the valley of the Esk may have been broken on this ancient gibbet. Some maiden toiling in the fields under the hot summer sun, in the parish of Danby, may have felt the pangs of dreadful anguish, hiding in secret her tears from those who knew not what her heart might know or feel. The morning sun of high hopes and expectations will have set darkly on this memorable place, where now we see only a stone post with its inscription, Gallow Howe.

To this unhallowed place in times long past, stealthily and in the sea hour of the night, the criminally minded will have come, coveting the dead malefactor's right hand, to be severed in haste from the arm of the body as it swung to and fro on the gibbet, perhaps under the clouded shadow of the hunter's or harvest moon. The owls, birds of the night, would be the only possible witnesses of this strange theft, as hurriedly but stealthily the wretch vanished with his coveted prize, which was to become, under his manipulation, a mysterious charm, dreaded of the dalesfolk, and known to them as the *Hand of Glory*.'

RAVEN.

© Mick Garratt

TURKEY NAB

A few miles due west across the hills at Turkey Nab another gibbet once stood on the nab of the high escarpment. Within sight of the ancient moorland route linking Ingleby Greenhow to Farndale, Bransdale and Kirkbymoorside, William Parkinson was the last to swing on the gallows there in 1729. His victim, a Scottish drover by the name of Archibald Noble. Parkinson's body was afterwards hung up in chains, presumably to deter others.[1]

---

1   *Daily Courant*, 1 Aug 1729. Criminal Chronology, p 45, www.yorkcastleprison.org.uk/family-history/condemned/hanged

REFERENCES

- *Some Reminiscences and Folk Lore of Danby Parish and District* by Joseph Ford, M.T.D. Rigg Publications, 1990
- 'William Parkinson and the gibbet on Turkey Nab', posted 28 June 2023 by Fhithich, www.fhithich.uk
- 'Ingleby Greenhow Heritage Leaflet: Kirby, Great Broughton & Ingleby Greenhaw', Local History Group, https://kgbighistory.org.uk

Moor Ghosts

GHOST OF WILLIAM PARKINSON?

I parked at Bank Foot, below Turkey Nab, said to derive from the local name for the grouse: wild turkeys. Or else it may come from Thurkilsti, the name of the ancient drovers' road from Kildale to Kirkbymoorside.[1] From Bank Foot the track winds up Ingleby Bank, circling past the nab...

I thought about William Parkinson, hung and gibbeted on this spot in 1729 for the murder of a Scottish drover at Great Broughton. He was tried at York assizes and brought back for the sentence to be carried out. All within fifteen days. Swift justice.

Later on my route I visited various sandstone outcrops and stones on Ingleby Moor and came across some verses on a piece of paper secreted away. These strangely resonated with my earlier thoughts of William Parkinson:

They hauled him to the crossroads
As day was at its close;
They hung him to the gallows
And left him for the crows.

His hands in life were bloody,
His ghost will not be still
He haunts the naked moorlands
About the gibbet hill.

And oft a lonely traveler
Is found upon the fen
Whose dead eyes hold a horror
Beyond the world of men.

The villagers then whisper,
With accents grim and dour:
'This man has met at midnight
The phantom of the moor.'

No title, no author. But back home Google came up trumps. They're from *The Moor Ghost* by Robert E. Howard, an American poet who as far as I can tell never visited England yet alone the North York Moors. Still, a weird coincidence. I wonder if whoever left the paper knew about William Parkinson.[2]

LADY MARY ROSS' SPECTRAL ODYSSEY

From this vantage point on Turkey Nab (photo below), one can just make out the rooftops of Ingleby Manor, nestled within that tongue of wood positioned slightly to the left of centre …

Ingleby Manor near Ingleby Greenhow, the seat of the Foulis family from 1608.

It's said that the spirit of Lady Mary Ross, mother to Lady Mary Foulis, has taken to haunting Ingleby Manor. The manor's website is the source of this spectral tale.[3] I must admit, my investigation has yielded no other mention of such ethereal occurrences.

In the realm of believing that a place might indeed harbour a ghost, one wonders why Lady Mary Ross would choose to revisit the living from beyond the grave in a place she never called home, never breathed her last, nor found her final resting place.

Certainly, in life, Lady Mary would have visited Ingleby Manor. Her daughter had, after all, tied the knot with Sir William Foulis, the Lord of the Manor at the time.

Nestled near a muddy track in a plantation overlooking Ingleby Manor, there is a seat hewn from a substantial boulder. It bears the inscription 'LADY MARY ROSS 1837' and is rumoured to mark her favoured path. It follows, then, that she must have visited her daughter fairly frequently.

Lady Mary Ross, wife of Sir Charles Lockhart-Ross 7th Baronet and mother of Lady Mary Foulis (the last Foulis heiress to the Ingleby Manor Estate). Mary Ross died in 1842.

| Lady Mary's Seat, Ingleby Manor Estate.

The year 1842 marked the passing of Lady Mary Ross. She had been wed to Sir Charles Lockhart-Ross, the 7th Baronet, whose family home was at Balnagowan in Ross-shire in the Scottish Highlands. And, lo-and-behold, overlooking the Balnagown River, there stands another commemorative seat dedicated to Lady Mary.[4] From what I can gather, this seat is not particularly obvious.[5]

Widowed when Sir Charles breathed his last in 1814, Lady Mary took on the mantle of de facto Laird at Balnagown. With her sole surviving son a mere toddler, she not only managed the extensive estate but also spearheaded numerous enhancements and expansions to the castle.[6]

Her final breath was drawn at her seat, Bonnington Castle, near Edinburgh, in 1842. A recent chill, acquired during her customary walks, coupled with lingering maladies, is reported to have hastened her demise. She found her final resting place at the Abbey of Fearn, the ancestral burial grounds of the Balnagown family. According to her obituary, she was well thought of by her tenantry and by *'the poor and destitute'*.[7]

Thus, the question lingers – why would she, in death, travel some 250 miles to haunt Ingleby Manor? Could there have been discord with Sir William Foulis and his mother-in-law, paving the way for spectral reprisals? But perhaps that is a little too cynical.

MICK GARRATT

---

1 Thurkilsti, or Thurkill's hill road, was mentioned in Walter Espec's grant of land to Rievaulx Abbey in 1145. This ancient route across the moors from Welburn and Skiplam descended at Turkey Nab on its way to Ingleby Greenhow and Stokesley (reference: 'Thurkilsti', 'Out and About on the North York Moors', 24 April 2017, www.fhithich.uk)
2 'Ghost of William Parkinson?' originally posted as 'Turkey Nab' by Fhithich, 3 January 2017 on his blog 'Out and About on the North York Moors…' www.fhithich.uk
3 Ingleby Manor, www.inglebymanor.co.uk
4 https://maps.nls.uk/view/75117355#zoom=5&lat=10869&lon=7616&layers=BT
5 'Lady Ann's Seat, Ross-Shire', A. Tryon, 2023, www.geograph.org.uk/photo/7576100
6 'Our History – Balnagown Estate', 2022, www.balnagown.com
7 'The Late Right Hon. Lady Mary Ross of Balnagown, John O' Groat Journal, Friday 14 October 1842, www.britishnewspaperarchive.co.uk

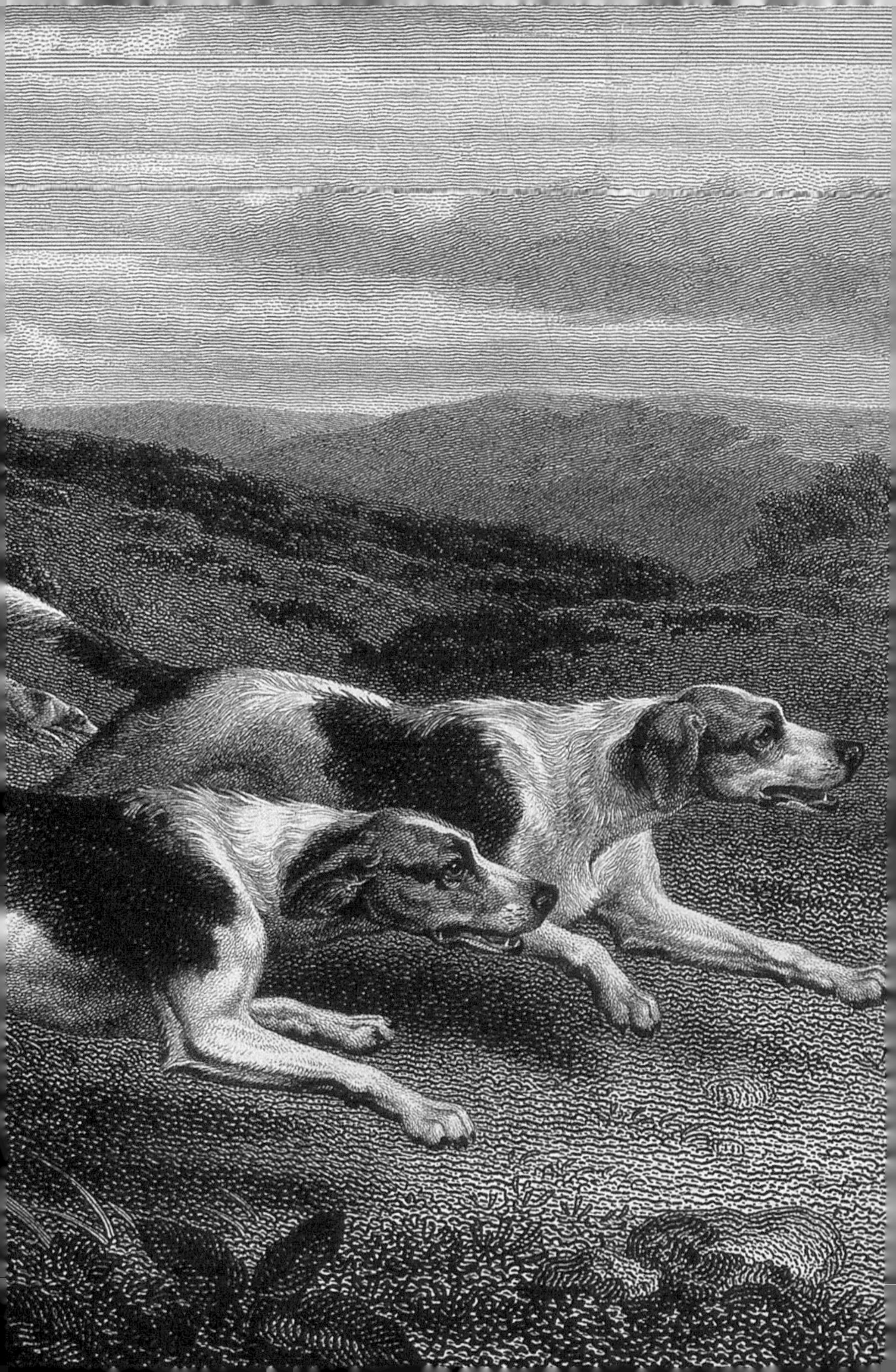

The Lockwood Beck Ghost Pack

This old tale from Mr R.J.M. Rascal of the Priory in Grosmont[1] relates to the area around Lockwood Beck reservoir, visible from the Guisborough to Whitby road.

During the Winter of 1914-1915, when my regiment, the 4th Battalion Green Howards was stationed at Cramlington in Northumberland, I went on leave to Whitby, where my parents were then living.

At the end of my leave, I motored back to Cramlington alone, and wanting to make full use of the short time allowed I did not set off on my journey until after dark.

It was a bright starry night without a sign of the fog which so often enshrouds the North Yorkshire Moors at that time of the year.

Leaving Whitby, I took the Guisboro' road. Today it is a fast main road, without the sharp corners and humped bridges which constituted such hazards in the early days of motoring. About half a mile before you reach the turn to Castleton and the Lockwood Beck, the road descends sharply down Lockwood Hill. In those days there was a large wood (Swindale Wood) on the North side, and on the South side was a thick fence. I was about half way down the hill, approaching the Hagg Beck, when five or six couple of hounds came out of the wood onto the road. As I jammed on the brakes, I realized I was among the pack and it seemed that I must have hit some of them. They appeared to be all round and underneath the car.

At that same moment the leading hounds disappeared through the fence on my right. I got out of the car, feeling sick with apprehension as to what I might find in the road. By the light of my headlamps I searched the roadside but to my amazement there was no sign of anything.

I stood still to listen, thinking that from the way in which hounds drove on over the road they must be close to their fox, and that on this still clear night I should surely hear their cry as they hunted on over the moor. But there was no sound.

Suddenly a feeling of fear overcame me.

I was alone on the Moor road, late at night and I realised that there could be no rational explanation of what had taken place. Although I had seen a pack of hounds I had heard nothing, nor had I felt any kind of bump or impact when I drove into the middle of the pack.

I had known Swindale Wood since I was a boy and had enjoyed many good hunts from there; now my one thought was to get away from it. All I wanted was to arrive as quickly as possible to the Mess at Cramlington where I would join my friends.

Next morning Colonel W.H.A. Wharton, who was my Commanding Officer and also Master of the Cleveland Hounds from 1886-1919, asked me what sort of drive back I had had the night before. I told him of my experience and he said at once, 'You have seen the Lockwood Beck Ghost Pack'.

---

1   Collected by the Countess of Feversham in *Strange Stories of the Chase* (1972) and spotted by Mick Garratt (www.fhithich.uk)

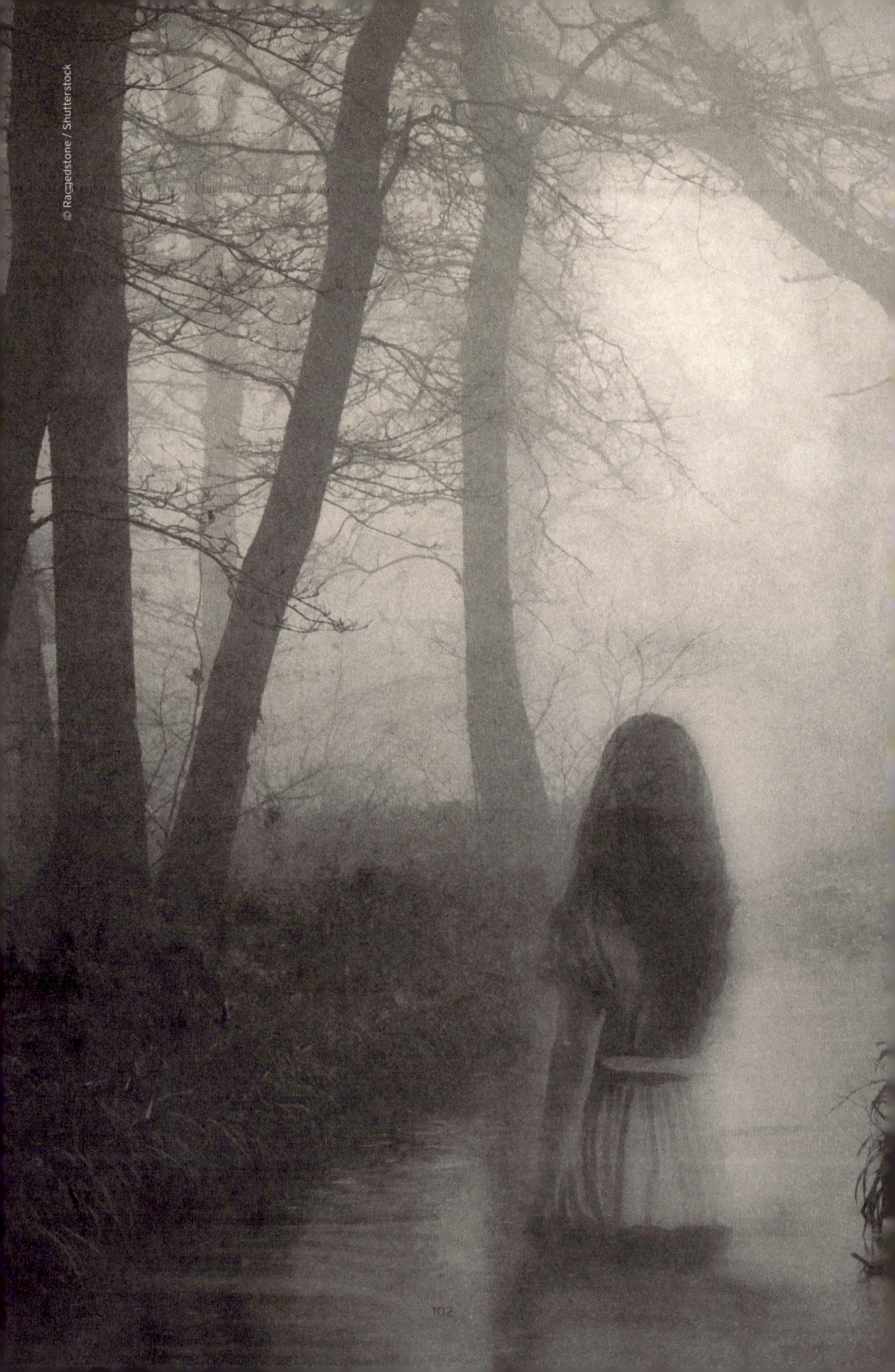

Following the Threads of Kitty and her Sark

Nowadays, the ghost story of Sarkless Kitty is a haunting moorland legend, capturing imaginations more than 225 years after the events on which it is based. Enigmatic and confusing, with a range of different versions now told, the story was almost certainly inspired by the deaths of real people. However, it's very difficult to unpick the points where fact and fiction meet.

Everyone is agreed that Kitty drowned in the 1780s at Lowna, a crossing place on the banks of the River Dove in Lower Farndale. Kitty's death was one of many at that spot, but in the narrative structure of the story of 'Sarkless Kitty' it is always the first death of the tale.

The story's name derives from Kitty's nakedness. A sark was a loose item of underclothing. In some versions of the story, her body was found wearing only the sark, which was removed for washing and laid out with her corpse before both her naked body and sark then apparently vanished. In other versions, Kitty's body was found naked, hence 'sarkless'. This is not necessarily surprising given the strength of the river.

At the time, Kitty was presumed to have taken her own life in great distress having been abandoned by her lover. In some versions of the story, Kitty was pregnant, though elsewhere she seems to have already had the child conceived out of wedlock. Following her own death, it was not long before Kitty's lover also drowned in the river and, over the succeeding two decades, multiple sightings of her naked ghost were reported. As the deaths of men crossing at the ford continued, Kitty's ghost was always blamed.

We know that some sort of 'exorcism' or ritual took place in 1807 or thereabouts, probably led by the Vicar of Lastingham. As a presumed suicide-victim, Kitty had not been allowed a Christian burial and so this service was said to have laid her to rest, putting a stop to the killings.

As early as the 1820s, a version of 'Sarkless Kitty's' story appeared in the Calvert Manuscript. Kitty was described as a 'bawdy wench' and 'the talk of these parts' by the age of 18 due to her physical attractiveness. In Calvert's manuscript, Kitty's story reads like the sort of morality tale that reinforced patriarchal values. Calvert described the struggles of Kitty's pious mother against her beautiful daughter's debauched tendencies in life, with crimes continuing even after death. Siren-like, Kitty's ghost allegedly used her beauty to call men to their deaths, or else startled their horses so that they reared as they crossed the river. However, Calvert did allow room for doubt by adding the words 'so we are told'.

The story continued to be elaborated and adapted over the years that followed. Characters were developed, names changed, and further mysterious details included. Then, during the 1980s, writer Peter Walker added his own theory that the real Kitty was perhaps not a victim of suicide but of murder at the hands of a lover unwilling to marry her. Any and all of this, of course, is impossible to prove.

By 1825, the ford at Lowna seems to have been considered dangerous enough when in spate to be replaced by a simple sandstone bridge. It has also been noted that many of the travellers who drowned there were strangers to the area and unlikely to be familiar with the perils of the river. However, by the time of Calvert's writing, Kitty's character had been fully assassinated. She was no longer a tragic victim but the ghostly perpetrator of a succession of killings.

ROSIE BARRETT

| The River Dove in Lower Farndale.

3

BELIEFS, RITUALS & TRADITIONS

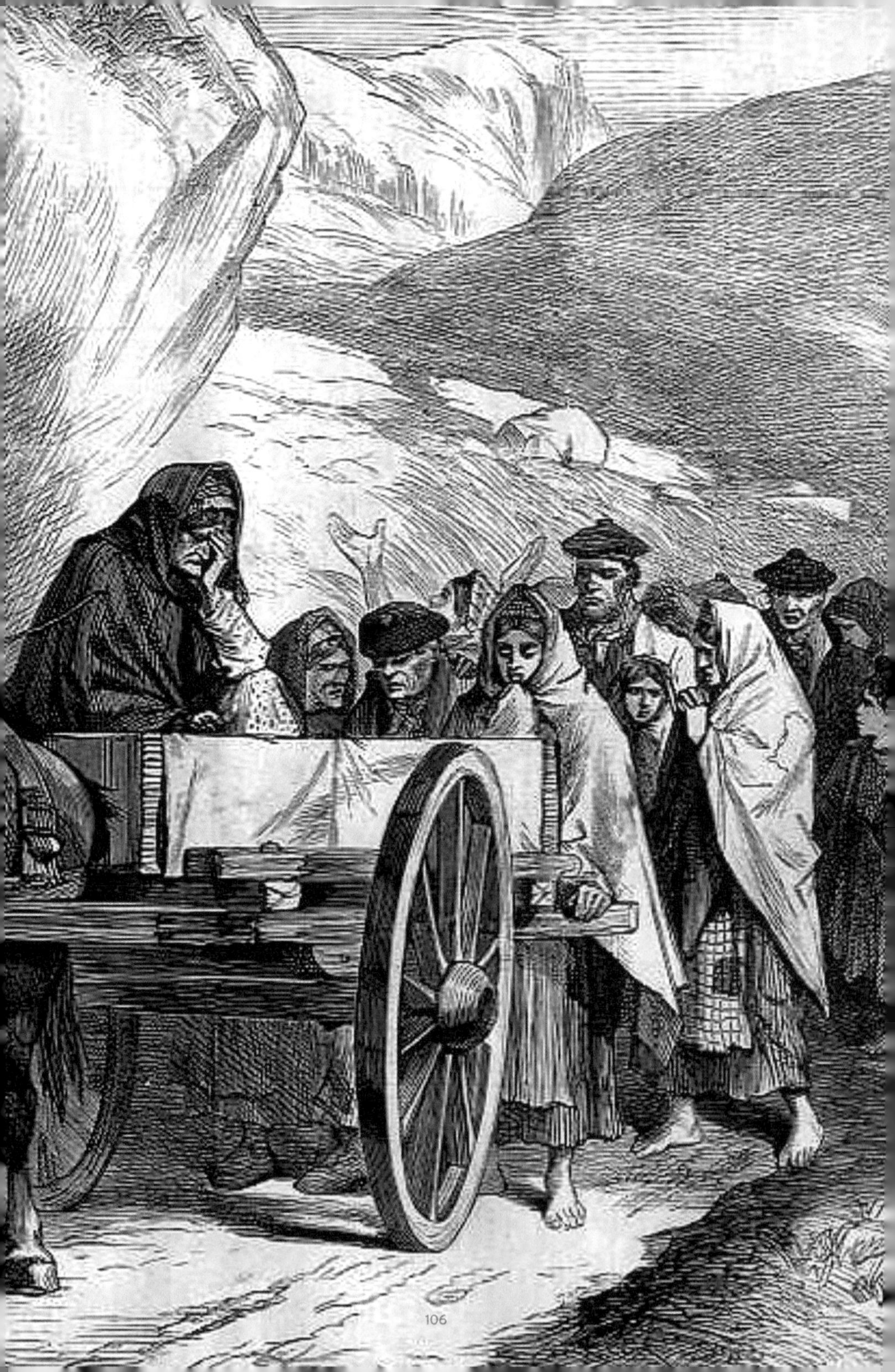

The Lyke Wake Walk... Inspired by a Song

The forty-mile Lyke Wake Walk follows the watershed of the North York Moors, from Scarth Wood Moor in the west to the coastal cliffs of Ravenscar at the eastern edge of the National Park. Its name was inspired by an ancient Yorkshire dialect song, the Lyke Wake Dirge, which tells of the soul's passage through the afterlife.

In 1955, Bill Cowley, a North Yorkshire farmer, local historian and journalist, wrote an article for the *Dalesman* magazine challenging walkers to cross the North York Moors on foot at its widest point from West to East within 24 hours. He described the route as *'on heather all the way except for when crossing one or two roads'*.

Bill successfully completed the first 'crossing' on 1 October 1955, setting off at noon with ten other men and two women, all of whom became founder members of the 'Lyke Wake Club'. Others joined later. Entry to the club was simply to complete the 'ordeal' of the crossing and receive a coffin badge and a 'condolence card' to prove it.

Scarth Wood Moor

© Mick Garratt

| The Wainstones on Hasty Bank

The challenge caught on and after fifty years had become a national legend, loved by seasoned walkers and newbies alike. During the 1960s and 1970s heydays, more than 160,000 completed the crossing – around 10,000 a year. Many think back to those times with nostalgia – the camaraderie, night-time adventure and blistered feet. Like the challenge walks of today, there was plenty of charitable fundraising too.

Glaisdale-born author Nicholas Rhea (1956–2017) recorded meeting the by-then famous Bill Cowley: *'a tall and slender man with a firm jawline and heavily-rimmed spectacles upon a very character-filled face. His strong voice was rich with the dialect of the moors, and he had an encyclopaedic knowledge of everything associated with the North York Moors, particularly the area around the Cleveland Hills.'*[1]

As the challenge acquired cult status, many thousands of copies of Cowley's guide were sold. *Lyke Wake Walk*[2] offers insights into the history, geography, natural history and folklore of the moorland route. Early editions, depicting the Club's coffin badge icon on the cover, can still be found second-hand.

During the first few years of the challenge, the walk followed an almost non-existent track, but by mid-1970s the large groups and sheer numbers of walkers had eroded an ever-expanding pathway that was disturbing fragile moorland ecology. The walk had to be re-thought.

| Bill Cowley

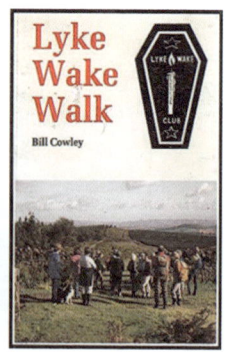

Ordnance Survey was told to remove the route from its maps and large groups were discouraged. The Lyke Wake Club worked with the National Park Authority and landowners to promote alternative routes, including the forty-mile 'Shepherd's Round', a circular from Sheepwash to Bloworth, Bransdale, Fangdale Beck, Hawnby and the Drove Road back to Sheepwash. Also, the thirty-two mile circular called the 'Hambleton Hobble', around Black Hambleton, from Osmotherley to Arden, Scawton, Boltby, Silton and back to Osmotherley.[3]

Challenge walks were becoming popular in other parts of the country, which helped to lessen the numbers walking the Lyke Wake Walk.

Following the death, in 1994, of Bill Cowley, 'Chief Dirger' and founder of the Lyke Wake Walk Club, it was agreed to wind up the Club. A last 'Golden Jubilee Wake' was planned at the Raven Hall Hotel, Ravenscar, in 2005, fifty years after the challenge had begun.[4] However, in 2004 a splinter group formed an unofficial 'New Lyke Wake Walk Club' dedicated to preserving the rituals begun by Bill, including celebrating multiple crossings with awards called degrees and an annual wake at Raven Hall Hotel, the popular end point for Lyke Wake 'dirgers'.

Today, the Lake Wake Walk is alive and well. Lower numbers walking the route have allowed the moorland to recover.

COFFIN TRAILS, FOLKLORE AND A DIRGE

Bill Cowley's name for his endurance challenge, 'Lyke Wake Walk', came from the Anglo-Saxon words 'lyke', meaning corpse, and 'wake' meaning watching over the deceased. A traditional lyke wake was the custom of watching over a body night and day from the person's last breath until burial.

Some say that the walk's name was simply Bill's humorous warning that towards the end of the Lyke Wake Walk you will feel like death. Others believe it refers to the old routes known as 'coffin trails' ('church/corpse' roads, or 'corpseways') that led from remote dale farm settlements to local churches. Coffins were carried along these routes for church burial. An example is the old corpse road from Fairy Cross in Fryup Dale across the rigg[5] to St Hilda's Church in Danby Dale – known as The Old Hell Way.[6]

'**The Lyke Wake Dirg**e' – sung in recent times on many Lyke Walk Walk occasions – is an ancient song in old Yorkshire dialect telling the story of the soul's travel, and hazards it faces, on its way from earth to purgatory. John Aubrey first recorded its existence as a poem in 1686 but noted that it was being sung in 1616 and was probably much older given its pre-Christian as well as Christian themes.

Folklorist Richard Blakeborough explains the significance of 'Whinny Moor' and the superstition that surrounds it:

'Although there is a place called Whinny Moor, as used in the Lyke Wake song, it is mythical, simply representing a wearying hindersome tract of land through which the soul must perforce pass, the ease or difficulty of such passage being lesser or greater according to the good deeds done and alms bestowed during life…

I cannot say when or where the Lyke Wake dirge was sung for the last time in the North Riding, but I remember once talking to an old chap who remembered it being sung over the corpse of a distant relation of his, a native of Kildale. This would be about 1800, and he told me that Lyke Wakes were of rare occurrence then, and only heard of in out-of-the-way places. Doubtless this was so, but a superstition closely connected with the Lyke Wake is still with us. Old people will tell you that after death the soul passes over Whinny Moor, a place full of whins and brambles; and according as the soul when a tenant of the body administered to the wants of others, so would its passage over the dreaded moor be made easy. It seems, according to the old belief, every one ought to give at least one pair of new shoes to some poor person, and as often as means would allow, feed and clothe the needy. Whether these rules were faithfully carried out or not, the soul on approaching Whinny Moor would be met by an old man carrying a huge bundle of boots; and if amongst these could be found a pair which the bare-footed soul had given away during life, the old man gave them to the soul to protect its feet whilst crossing the thorny moor.'[7]

NICOLA CHALTON

The Lyke Wake Dirge

This ae nighte, this ae nighte,
   (Refrain) *Every nighte and alle,*
Fire and fleet[8] and candle-lighte,
   (Refrain) *And Christe receive thy saule.*

When thou from hence away art past,
To Whinny-muir thou com'st at last;

If ever thou gavest hosen and shoon,
Sit thee down and put them on;

If hosen and shoon thou ne'er gav'st nane
The whinnes will prick thee to the bare bane;

From Whinny-muir when thou may'st pass,
To Brig o' Dread[9] thou com'st at last;

From Brig o' Dread when thou may'st pass,
To Purgatory fire thou com'st at last;

If ever thou gavest meat or drink,
The fire shall never make thee shrink;

If meat or drink thou ne'er gav'st nane,
The fire will burn thee to the bare bane;

This ae nighte, this ae nighte,
   Every nighte and alle,
Fire and fleet and candle-lighte,
   And Christe receive thy saule.

from the *Oxford Book of English Verse* (1900)

---

1. Read the full article, 'Nicholas Rhea remembers Bill Cowley', at: www.lykewake.org/cowley.php
2. Cowley, Bill (1959), *Lyke Wake Walk: Forty Miles Across the North Yorkshire Moors,* Dalesman Books
3. Walk leaflets/books, alternative routes, information and badges for those who complete the walk are available from the official Lyke Wake Walk Club website: www.lykewakewalk.co.uk/history.html
4. A photographic record of the Lyke Wake Club history is held at the Ryedale Folk Museum
5. Rigg – Ridge
6. 'Wandering Over Danby Rigg', August 15, 2020, https://teessidepsychogeography.wordpress.com/category/corpse-road
7. *Wit, Character, Folklore and Customs of the North Riding of Yorkshire* by Richard Blakeborough (1911)
8. 'Fire and fleet' commonly used in early wills to refer to house and home
9. Bridge of Dread – a bridge to Purgatory that a dead soul has to cross; evil souls fall from the bridge into hell

FURTHER READING
- *Old Roads & Pannierways in North East Yorkshire*, R. H. Hayes (1988), The North York Moors National Park

Corn Dollies

✦ Our ancestors used magical thinking to attempt to control the harvest. Rituals around the last sheaf have likely been practised for thousands of years.

Each year, tradition held that a corn dolly be made with the last sheaf of corn at the end of harvest. The dolly was kept inside to be ritualistically ploughed back into the soil when sowing recommenced. This act was originally thought to promote fertility for the next planting season, but it is likely that the tradition continued long after the magical thinking had faded.

As with many other rural crafts, corn dolly making experienced a revival during the 1960s and 1970s. Once harvesting had become mechanised, the corn produced was no longer suitable for making dollies. By that point, of course, the ritualistic purpose of corn dollies had already faded along with magical thinking more generally.

The craft of corn dolly making continues today due to the efforts of individual crafters who have sought to preserve this heritage. Their corn dollies are appreciated as impressive works of art.

© Ryedale Folk Museum

Westerdale's Corn Spirits & Corn Dollies

Emma Beeforth (1920–2017) lived for more or less all of her years in Westerdale, the most westerly dale of the Esk Valley. She grew up in a household where sewing was often undertaken. Her mother liked to do patchwork and quilting so there was often a quilting frame set up in the living room once they were at Ivy Holme. However, Emma particularly enjoyed embroidery and during the 1970s she joined an embroidery class held one evening a week at Castleton Village Hall. Along with a number of other local ladies she learned about satin stitch, chain stitch, French knots and all of the other embroidery stitches. Emma of course had to pack her work into a basket and walk all the way to Castleton and then all the way back again to Westerdale after her evening of sewing but she thoroughly enjoyed this time. And her work was of the highest standard. The usual practice is to pull threads through to the back of the work in order to fasten off and there is a definite right and wrong side but Emma was so meticulous and careful about this that her work was as neat on the back as it was on the front. It really was of Embroiderers' Guild standard and the other ladies readily acknowledged her skill.

| Emma and Sid at home with some of their corn dollies.

As well as embroidery, Emma, like most women at the time, did knitting and dressmaking and was used to mending, but there was one particular and rather unusual craft that she and her husband Sid were to become famous for and that was making corn dollies.

Corn dolly making is an old custom with a very long history. In the days before mechanised harvesting and a scientific understanding of the natural world there was a great deal of folklore attached to harvest time. People believed that the spirit of the corn lived within the crop and that the harvest in effect made this homeless. A corn dolly was formed from the last sheaf of straw so that the corn spirit could live on and would be ploughed into the field when the next year's crop was sown. By the time Sid and Emma were becoming interested in corn dolly making the folklore was losing its power but the craft itself had become a celebrated art form.

As an aspect of his role on the farm, Sid made the straw structures as part of the harvest tradition. Initially these were simple figures but he and Emma then acquired two books on corn dolly making and for many years enjoyed sharing the craft of weaving straw into the most wonderful shapes. Although they had these books of designs they were both keen to develop their own and Emma would lie awake at night wondering how to make a particular item. An elaborate cornucopia, baskets, crosses as well as letters became her hallmark. Emma even managed to fashion a royal crown and Stephenson's Rocket. The only thing she could never master was to make a horse, even though she puzzled over it for a long time. She just couldn't fathom out how to do that but she did make a cart and then bought a plastic horse for the shafts. For many years these corn dollies were a feature of the Mell Supper held in Westerdale Village Hall.

Knowing that this craft was dying out, Emma was keen to teach others and she and Sid would take their straw and give demonstrations at the Ryedale Folk Museum. They also went to the historic Clarke Hall in Wakefield with the children of Castleton School. For these events they would usually dress up in period costume looking like a nineteenth-century farmer and his wife. It was all a lot of fun – if it did leave the living room in rather a mess.

It was in later years that Emma developed a love of, and an excellent reputation for, rug making. People in country communities often made rag

| Sid and Emma at Ryedale Folk Museum, 1978.

Sid making a corn dolly.

rugs, or clippy mats, out of discarded clothes, especially old suiting. Many of us will remember them as a feature of childhood. The 'rags' were short strips, about half an inch wide, with both ends pushed into the wrong side of hessian sacking. The result is literally a raggy rug. However, Emma's trademark became hooky rugs. These are made with long strips of cloth woven into the right side of the base canvas with the use of a latched hook. The result is a smooth mat and Emma became very adept at these, making them for herself but also to sell to raise money for church funds. First she would draft a design – usually using the back of a cereal packet – and then transfer the final pattern onto the hessian. A colour scheme had to be chosen and then old jumpers, suits or whatever was to hand were cut into long narrow strips. This was the painstaking part but Emma simply soldiered on. She had boxes and boxes of balls of strips ready for rug making. However, if she was not able to find something suitable for her design then she would set to and dye an old discarded garment or piece of cloth in order to complete the work.

Emma continued to make rugs into her mid-nineties: even at that age and after so many years of practice her hands allowed her to manipulate the hook and guide the strips into it. Scorched occasionally with a spark from the fire, the rug in her own living room had been down on the floor for several decades doing service as a hearth rug. There will be many more still in use that are testament to her skill.

CAROL M. WILSON

Extract from Carol M. Wilson's book *The Life of Emma Beeforth (1920-2017)*, published in 2020. Images from Emma's photograph albums, courtesy of her family.

Here We Come A Wassailing

Wassailing is an old English custom of midwinter, especially associated with Christmas and New Year. It was usually celebrated on Twelfth Night (5 or 6 January) or 'Old Twelfth Night' (17 January).

The ritual probably dates back to Anglo-Saxon times but the term 'wassail' is from the middle ages, derived from 'Waes Hael',[1] from Middle English, meaning 'be in good health' – borrowed from the Old Norse salvation 'ves heill'. The usual response was 'Drink Hael', meaning 'drink and be healthy'.

In medieval times, feudal lords gave peasants food and drink in exchange for the peasants' blessing delivered in the form of a wassail song. The peasants' song was not considered to be begging but a sign of goodwill.

In later times, wassailing took two forms: visiting neighbours to drink and sing (now largely overtaken by carol singing) and wassailing the orchards to encourage a good harvest.

The Wassail Bowl by John Gilbert, 1860.

YORKSHIRE WASSAIL SONG

North Yorkshire's carol singing customs have long roots in the wassailing tradition. Children (and later, all ages) typically went from door to door singing Christmas songs, the hosts rewarding them with gifts of money, food or heated spice cider or beer (known as wassail) to warm them up.

In return the singers would bless their hosts and remind them to pray for those who had 'wandered in the mire' (i.e. sinned – a mire was a bog, of which there were plenty in Northern parts).

The Yorkshire Wassail Song was the most widely known of all the Wassail songs. Versions varied from Yorkshire village to village; the one below dates back to the fifteenth century and appeared in *Christmas Carols New and Old* in 1871:

We've been a-while a-wandering,
Amongst the leaves so green.
But now we come a wassailing,
So plainly to be seen.

For it's Christmas time, when we travel far and near,
May God bless you and send you a happy New Year.

We are not daily beggars,
That beg from door to door,
But we are neighbours' children,
Whom you have seen before.

For it's Christmas time, when we travel far and near,
May God bless you and send you a happy New Year.

We've got a little purse,
Made of stretching leathern skin.
We want a little money,
To line it well within.

For it's Christmas time, when we travel far and near,
May God bless you and send you a happy New Year.

Call up the butler of this house,
Put on his golden ring.
Let him bring us out a glass of beer,
The better we shall sing.

For it's Christmas time, when we travel far and near,
May God bless you and send you a happy New Year.

So bring us out a table,
And spread it with a cloth,
And bring us out a mouldy cheese,
And then your Christmas loaf.

For it's Christmas time, when we travel far and near,
May God bless you and send you a happy New Year.

WASSAILING THE ORCHARDS

In different regions of the country, especially cider-producing areas, it was the custom to wassail the orchards on what was known as 'Old Twelvey' (17 January). Children and adults would visit an orchard, encircle the largest tree, and sing:

Stand fast, bear well top,
Pray God send us a howling crop;
Every twig, apples big;
Every bough, apples enow,
Hats full, caps full,
Full quarter sacks full.

"Here's to thee, old apple-tree,
Whence thou may'st bud, and thou may'st blow!
And whence thou may'st bear apples enow!
Hats full! caps full!
Bushel—bushel—sacks full!
And my pockets full too! Huzza!"

Then they would rap the trees with their sticks.[2] Some were known to fire off gunpowder under the trees to ensure a good crop, the object being to scare away evil spirits that might harm the fruit.[3] A good crop was in the interests of both the labourers, who were typically partly paid in apple cider, and the landlords, who needed plentiful produce to attract dependable workers.

Traditional wassailing ceremonies at orchards might include:

• A wassail king or queen leading a procession of singers and musicians from one orchard to the next.

• The king or queen being lifted into the boughs of a tree to place a piece

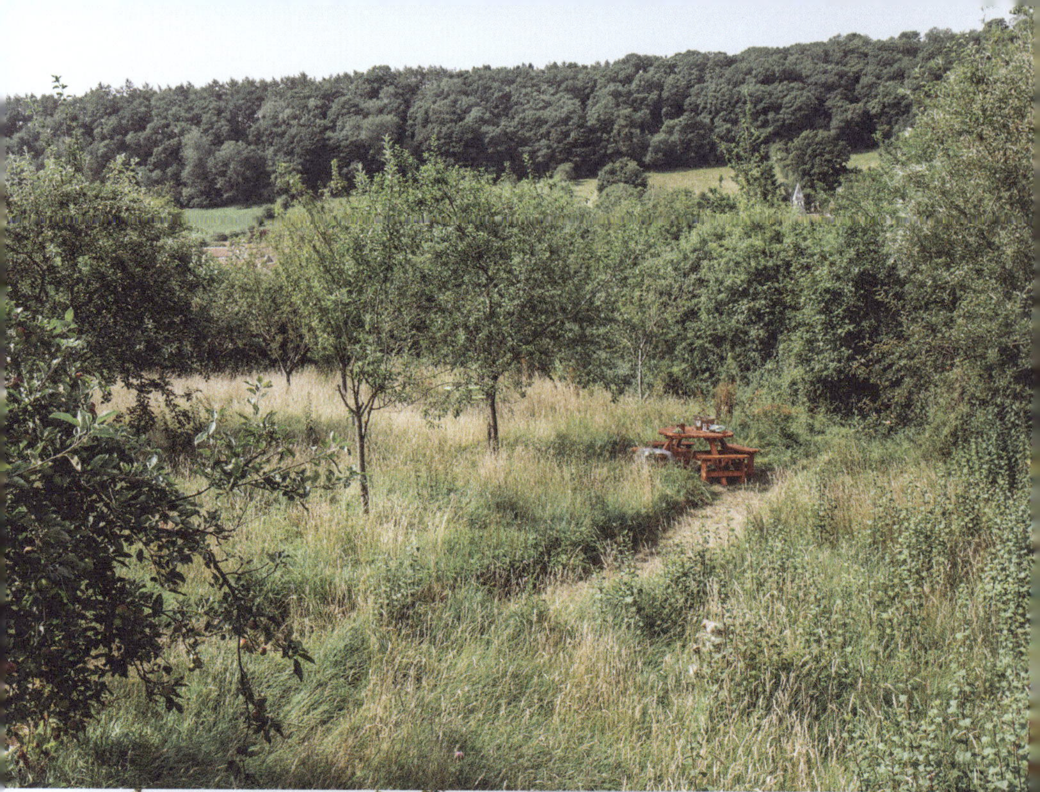

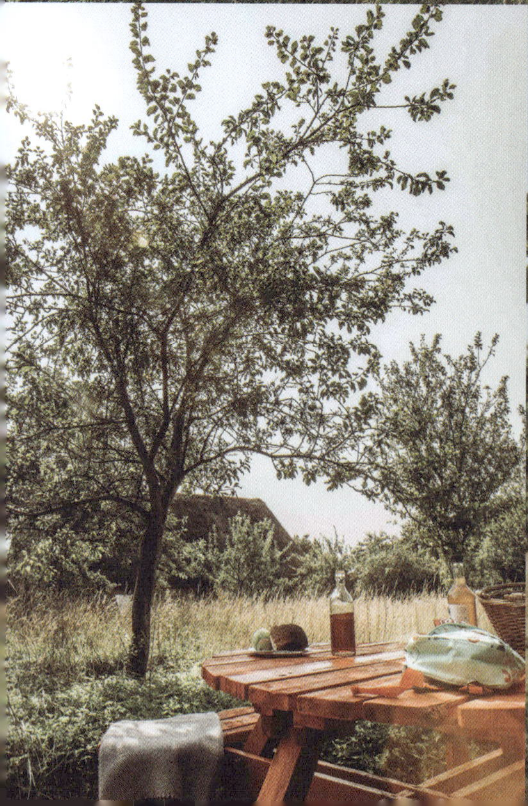

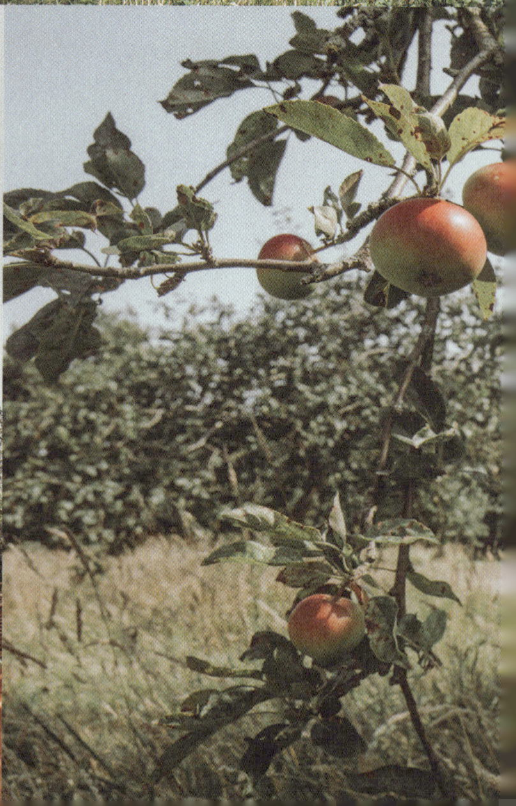

of toast soaked from the wassail bowl as a gift to the tree (or to the robins, symbols of spring song, good fortune and a conduit to the spirit world).
- Cider from the wassailing bowl being poured over the roots of the trees.
- The company reciting an incantation, for example:
Here's to thee old apple tree, Whence thou may'st bud, and thou may'st blow, And whence thou may'st bear apples enow! Hats full, caps full, bushel bushel sacks full! And my pockets full too! Huzzah!
- Pots and pans being clattered to ward off evil spirits and awaken the trees from winter slumber.
- Serenading of the trees with traditional songs followed by dancing.
A-wassail, a-wassail!
The Moon, she shines down;
The apples are ripe and the nuts they are brown.
Whence thou mayest bud, dear old apple tree,
And whence thou mayest bear, we sing unto thee.

Wassailing on Twelfth Night, c. 1863.

Some communities today are reviving the tradition of wassailing the orchards to celebrate nature, local fruit-growing and the old customs. Pagan pageantry re-enacted at these events serves as a reminder of the magical thinking of old.

NICOLA CHALTON

> **Lamb's Wool**, a typical concoction for the wassail bowl, consisted of roasted apples, sugar, nutmeg, ginger and wine or ale; the soft apple floating on top looked like lamb's wool, hence the name. During wassail ceremonies, adults and children eat spiced cake and each, in turn, took a roasted apple from the wassail bowl by means of a spoon, then drank to the health of the company.
>
> Nighttime festivities marking the end of Christmas holidays in the North of England often featured Lamb's Wool, along with dancing and a communal dinner of Lobscouse - a stew of beef, potatoes and onions.[4]

---

1   Oxford English Dictionary
2   *Old English Sports*, P.H. Ditchfield, 1891
3   *British Calendar Customs*, Vol II: Fixed Festivals, A.R. Wright, 1938
4   ibid

Whitby's Ceremony of the Penny Hedge

Of all the local folk customs, none is more inexplicably odd than the strange ritual, the Penny Hedge ceremony, which occurs in Whitby harbour on the morning of every Ascension Eve (the day before Ascension Day), exactly six weeks after Easter. The origins of the ceremony are lost in the mists of time; but, amazingly, there is documentary evidence showing that the custom existed as long as nine hundred years ago.

What happens is as follows: the Bailiff of the Manor Court of Fylingdales (and it *has* to be Fylingdales) arranges on Ascension Eve morning the collection from the surrounding district of branches and stems of hazel, known as '*stowers*' and '*yethers*'. At low tide, these are pounded into the mud flats of the harbour, and woven together, in order to create a short hedge some four feet in height by some six feet in length. The ceremony is always witnessed by a gaggle of curious onlookers. The climax of the event comes when an ancient hunting horn is produced and sounded across the harbour, echoing that the ritual has been successfully completed. Immediately following this, the Fylingdales Bailiff bawls across the harbour as loudly as he can: '*out on ye, out on ye, out on ye*', and the ceremony is quickly brought to an end. The words '*out on ye*' are a thrice-repeated plea to the elements that the hedge should withstand at least three tides (meaning, possibly, three seasonal high tides), without being washed away by any unwelcome current.

There are two contrasting explanations for the origins of the ceremony: the first is a folk tale, in which the hedge is seen as a penance for some misdeed committed by local gentry – in other words it was a Penance Hedge, and descendants of those families involved in the original misdeed were obliged to continue the annual ceremony, in perpetuity. It was understood at one time that if the hedge tragically failed and gave way before 'three tides' had elapsed, then those families involved in the hedge construction might be in danger of losing their lands held under Whitby Abbey. The families involved were obviously anxious to maintain the success of the custom, generation after generation, in order to preserve their ownership of valued inherited property.

Watercolour painting of the Ceremony by Richard Green.

The second explanation puts forwards the theory that the hedge was once a fishing weir, in which fish which had drifted up the Esk by the tide were caught in the 'hedge' as the tide receded. If this were the case, then the structure would have been considerably longer and more substantial than the one seen each year these days. It might have stretched out from the southern shore by some thirty feet or more.

The maintenance and repair of this once important facility, owned by the nearby Abbey, appears to have been the duty of a small and select group of local residents, the half-a-dozen freeholders, mainly members of the local gentry. It was *only* representatives of these exclusive freeholding families who had the responsibility, tedium and expense of carrying out the ceremony annually.

The names of various families who were for generations bound up in the hedge obligation included the Percies of Dunsley, the Conyers of Bagdale, the Etheringtons of Ugglebarnby, the Strangeways of Sneaton, and the Allatsons of Harton House, Fyling Raw. All but one of these were families of gentry status; it is also likely they had a common ancestor – perhaps one of the Percies – perhaps even the original William de Percy who re-founded Whitby Abbey in c.1100. All but one of these families managed to extinguish their obligation to prevail with the annual chore – no doubt by a considerable down payment. In the end, only the Allatsons of Fyling Raw were left, possibly because, as yeoman farmers with only a relatively small amount of freehold land, about 40 acres, they simply did not have sufficient funds to rid themselves of the duty. This explains why it is the role of whoever is Bailiff of Fylingdales to continue the ceremony to this day: the Bailiff would have always administered the freehold obligations attached to '*Allatson's antient oxgang*' at Harton House Farm through the Fyling Court Leet.

The legend of a supposed misdeed by gentry ancestors is far more colourful, but it has been ridiculed by medieval scholars for its confusion of names and dates which do not relate to reality. The folk legend tells of a group of local gentlemen – yes, the Percies, Strangeways, Conyers and so forth – who were pursuing a boar during a local hunt near Eskdale Hermitage. The boar took refuge within the Hermitage, and the elderly priest dwelling there refused to let the hunters have their quarry. In response, the huntsmen angrily attacked the priest, beat him up, and injured him severely. The priest ultimately died from his wounds, but not without forgiving his attackers. Following his death, a punishment was meted out to his assailants: not the death penalty, not imprisonment, nor a heavy fine, but the 'penance' of carrying out the Penny Hedge Ceremony annually in Whitby harbour, an obligation which descendants of the violent perpetrators of the crime were compelled to continue in perpetuity. The lack of logic in this story lies in the fact that it would have been highly unfair to have imposed such a continuing penalty on innocent and law-abiding descendants of those originals who had supposedly committed the crime.

Nevertheless, we must not forget the long narrow field forming part of the Allatson's old farm at Harton House, Raw, named West Bank, running alongside Katerham beck. There is a strong local tradition that this was actually the field where the boar hunt in question started all those centuries ago. Recent owners of the farm, when they sold it, made a point of retaining this field in their continuing possession because of the significance to them of its historical, sentimental and folk connections. Intuitively, we feel that there must be some grain of truth in the legend of the manslaughter of the monk; but exactly how this relates to a probable medieval fishing weir on the Esk remains an unanswered question.

ALASTAIR LAURENCE

For more in-depth coverage of this topic, see Alastair Laurence's book *The Penny Hedge, a Whitby Rustic Oddity* (2024).

ACKNOWLEDGEMENT
Alastair Laurence is grateful to Dr Tom Pickles of the Department of Medieval History, University of Chester, who was the first to suggest that the Penny Hedge could have begun life as a fishing weir.

The Foretelling of Thunder

This poem was given to George Calvert of Kirkbymoorside by John Holliday of Castlegate in the early nineteenth century.

When the Thunder's loud crack
Shakes the Heavenly vaults
Tis the Lord wheea is calling
To mankind o' their faults.

When it Thunders on God's day
Among those learned come death
Then some judge or Great General
Will soon gasp for breath.

Monday's Thunder fore mid-day
Holds great ladies in thrall
But a crack heard at Sunset
Brings a King's wench to fall.

Tuesday's Thunder sends luck
May it Thunder amain
It fetches mair gear[1]
And it biggens all grain.

True Wednesday's Thunder
Comes black loud and long
And Hell wark death geokens[2]
All harlots among.

Thursday's Thunder at t'backend[3]
When tups[4] play their pairt
Gives good hold to the yows[5]
To the grain a good heart.

Friday's Thunder from Hellwards
Does hang a black pall
Over Council and King
Death slaftering all.

Should the storm then hang over
While Setterday morning
There'll be plagues and sad deather
O' dree work naught be shorn.

---

1   goods, money or cattle
2   scoffs or laughs at
3   end of the year - winter
4   rams
5   ewes

Here We Go Round… the Kissing Ring

The Kissing Ring, once practised in the North York Moors, was claimed to be an ancient fertility rite. But what exactly was it? Ryedale Folk Museum's founder, Bert Frank, took part in a Kissing Ring in 1930 following the Rudland Chapel Anniversary. It was possibly the last time this rite was performed in these parts.

On a moonlit night, Bert recalled, some 40 young people joined hands and circled in a glade of trees.

The evening sounds elemental, with dramatic sheet lightning accompanying their chant. Some recalled the old belief that their actions would ripen the corn.

After a time, the ring diminished as couples broke away, the boys escorting the girls home to their farms.

He recalled these words which are said to be one possible Kissing Ring song:

A KISSING RING SONG

King Henry was King James's son
And all the royal races ran
Upon his heart he wears a star
Right away to the ocean far
So choose to the East
And choose to the West
And choose the one that you love the best
If he's not there to take her part
Choose another with all your heart.

How to Find Your Valentine

Traditional rituals collected from Yorkshire and Cleveland over a hundred years ago include this practice for young maids to find the person they might one day marry.

Take one of your own garters (perhaps a sock would do) and place a key within the Bible, resting on the page Ruth i. verses 16, 17. Close the Bible and bind it securely by winding the garter round the outside, then suspend the garter and Bible from a nail.

Seat yourself facing your assistant (a close friend), each of you placing an elbow on the table and resting the visible part of the key against your index fingers. Now name several of your male acquaintances and the key will turn when the name of your future husband is uttered.

To find out when you will be married, take a looking-glass and an apron which you have never worn before or held between yourself and the light, and go into the garden when the moon is full. Do not look at the moon. Keeping your back to the moon, stand upon something you have never stood on before — a newspaper, an old box, anything — and draw the apron over the glass, holding it so that the moon shines upon it. Now count the number of moons you see reflected through the apron, and this will be the number of years before the happy day arrives. Tip: if you are in a violent hurry to get married, it is best to choose an apron of light material, and to draw it tightly over the glass; careful attention to these details has a marvellous tendency to lessen the number of moons.

To discover whether you will be married or die an 'old maid': from a stream running southwards, fill a clean glass with water, borrow an old wedding ring and attach it to a single hair drawn from your own head. Rest your elbow on the table and hang the ring over the glass of water, suspended from the hair laid across the ball of your thumb. Should the ring hit the side of the glass, your fate is sealed – you will die an old maid; if, however, it spins round quickly, you will have to wait a year; if slowly, you will be wedded more than once.

It is commonly held that if you can find a four-leaved clover, and then walk backwards upstairs to bed, and sleep with the leaf under your pillow, you will dream of the man you will marry.

REFERENCE
- *Wit, Character, Folklore and Customs of the North Riding of Yorkshire* (1911), Richard Blakeborough

Sword Dancing

Like Morris dancing, sword-dancing celebrations have been much debated by historians and folklorists.

At times during the twentieth century, some folklorists were tempted to trace the origins of sword dancing from Neolithic rites to awaken the earth from its winter sleep. It's easy to see why they have been interpreted this way. These dances took place in rural areas where life was at the mercy of the whims of the harvest.

However, this theory of Pagan origins is now largely discounted. They have been traced as far back as 1777 in this country, when antiquary John Brand recorded seeing the 'lock' formation in Tyneside, and to the fourteenth century in the Netherlands.

It is most likely that the dances were a way to raise income for labouring men in need of sustenance during the winter months.

Longsword Dancing in the Esk Valley and East Cleveland

English Longsword is a dance tradition with its roots in Yorkshire – although its origins are uncertain and have been the subject of many theories over the years, some plausible and some highly implausible. One theory is that the dance came here with the Saxons or the Danes, which does have some merit as the prevalence of sword dancing does accord with the areas colonised by these settlers. It is unlikely that anybody will ever know for sure.

The dances are performed by teams of six or eight men and the custom was a mid-winter one, with Boxing Day and Plough Monday (the first Monday after twelfth night) being the favoured days, although some teams toured the surrounding area for a week or more before Christmas, basically as a way of collecting money when the chances of employment were curtailed.

The dance itself comprises some intricate movements going under and over the swords culminating in the making of a 'lock' or 'rose' when the swords are intertwined and held up for display. The swords themselves are generally metal strips three foot or a metre in length with a wooden handle at one end and were never swords in the military sense.

A number of longsword dance teams were once to be found in the Esk Valley area, chief among them were Sleights and Goathland – Goathland is the only team still dancing, with a history going back to the early part of the nineteenth century. Not too far away, in the ironstone mining area of East Cleveland, a number of teams existed from the late nineteenth century right up until the late 1960s. Brotton, Lingdale, Boosbeck, Loftus, Skelton, North Skelton and Skelton Green all had teams. Some readers may even remember being taught the dances at school during the 1940s and 50s.

Until the end of the nineteenth century and the first decade of the twentieth, rural traditions received little attention in published media and if it wasn't for a few dedicated folklore collectors many of them would have died out completely and gone unrecorded.

In the 1960s, however, there was an upsurge in the interest in our native folk song and dance, which lead to the formation of a number of 'revival' teams nationally, many of them choosing to perform the North Skelton dance. One such team was formed by members of the 'Cutty Wren' Folksong Club based in Redcar in 1967. Redcar Sword Dancers, as they called themselves, chose to learn the Greatham Sword Dance, which is interesting in being one of the very few longsword dances from County Durham and also in that it also has a short play embedded in the dance during which one of the characters is killed and brought back to life. Redcar still perform this tradition on Boxing Day in the village of Greatham on the outskirts of Hartlepool. Some of the other dance traditions also had plays but these have either been lost or are simply no longer enacted.

This has been a very brief outline of one of our local traditions, but if you wish to learn more a quick search on the internet for 'longsword dancing' will ring up many examples both in this country and abroad.

BRIAN PEARCE

The Goathland Plough Stots

The Goathland Plough Stots, a traditional Yorkshire longsword team, are still going strong. The team is one of the oldest still dancing their own dance as performed as far back as the early nineteenth century.

After a lapse of forty years the Plough Stots were revived by Frank W. Dowson in the 1920s, from local memory and with the help of his good friend Cecil Sharp. Two years after their search for manuscripts the Plough Stots danced their first outing in January 1923. Their outings over the last hundred years have taken them far and wide, and in recent times to the International Sword Spectacular in 2004 and the Czech Republic in 2005.

The Plough Stots dance five dances, each with an accompanying tune. These five dances require a team of six sword dancers, however there is a sixth dance which uses a further two dancers ('No Man's Jig'). Each of the dances results in the dancers weaving their swords into a 'lock'.

Accompanying the dancers is a gentleman called 'Old Isaac', a 'fool' and the musicians. This ritual began in Pagan times when the young men were pulling the plough and a play came into being. In time a 'Gentleman' and 'Lady' appeared at the head of the company, then the collectors ('Toms'), and

Goathland Plough Stots at the Royal Albert Hall with Eliza Carthy.

an old couple 'Isaac' and 'Betty' ('T'awd man and T'awd Woman') bringing up the rear.

Today, the musicians consist of fiddle and accordian players. The team is honoured to have Eliza Carthy as fiddle player.

The dancers wear a uniform of pink and blue tunics tied with a white sash and grey trousers with red stripes. Youth team members also adopt this uniform but instead of tunics they wear pink and blue tabards. The tunic colours of pink and blue were chosen to placate the political parties of the nineteenth century (Whigs and Tories), whilst the red stripe on the trousers is a remnant of the Crimean War.

When Goathland Plough Stots dance out it is traditional for a song to be sung before they start:

We're Gooadlan Pleeaf Stots com'd ageaan
All decked wi' ribbons fair
Seea noo we'll do the best we can
An' the best can deea neea mair.

The longer version, as sung by Keith Thompson at The Royal Albert Hall and on other special occasions, goes like this:

Here's a host of us all
From Goathland go we
We're goin a rambling
The country for to see
The country for to see
Some pass-time for to take
So freely you will give to us
As freely we will take
So now you see us all
Dressed in our fine array
Think of us what you will
Music strike up and play.

The Reading Room in Goathland (built in 1884) housed an exhibition of the Plough Stots' dance memorabilia for many years. After the village lost its mobile library service, Keith Thompson and other Plough Stot and village members fundraised for the new Goathland Community Hub and Sports Pavilion, which opened in 2017. This multi-functional building provides a large indoor area for community activities with space for exhibitions, a library, performances, sports meetings and for the longsword dancers to continue their tradition.

Thank you to Keith Thompson for permission to base this article on material from the Goathland Plough Stots' website (www.goathlandploughstots.com).

You can watch a 1939 film of the Dance of the Goathland Plough Stots on YouTube at https://youtu.be/IWtRLLP_3t0

Plough Monday:
An Old Yorkshire Tradition

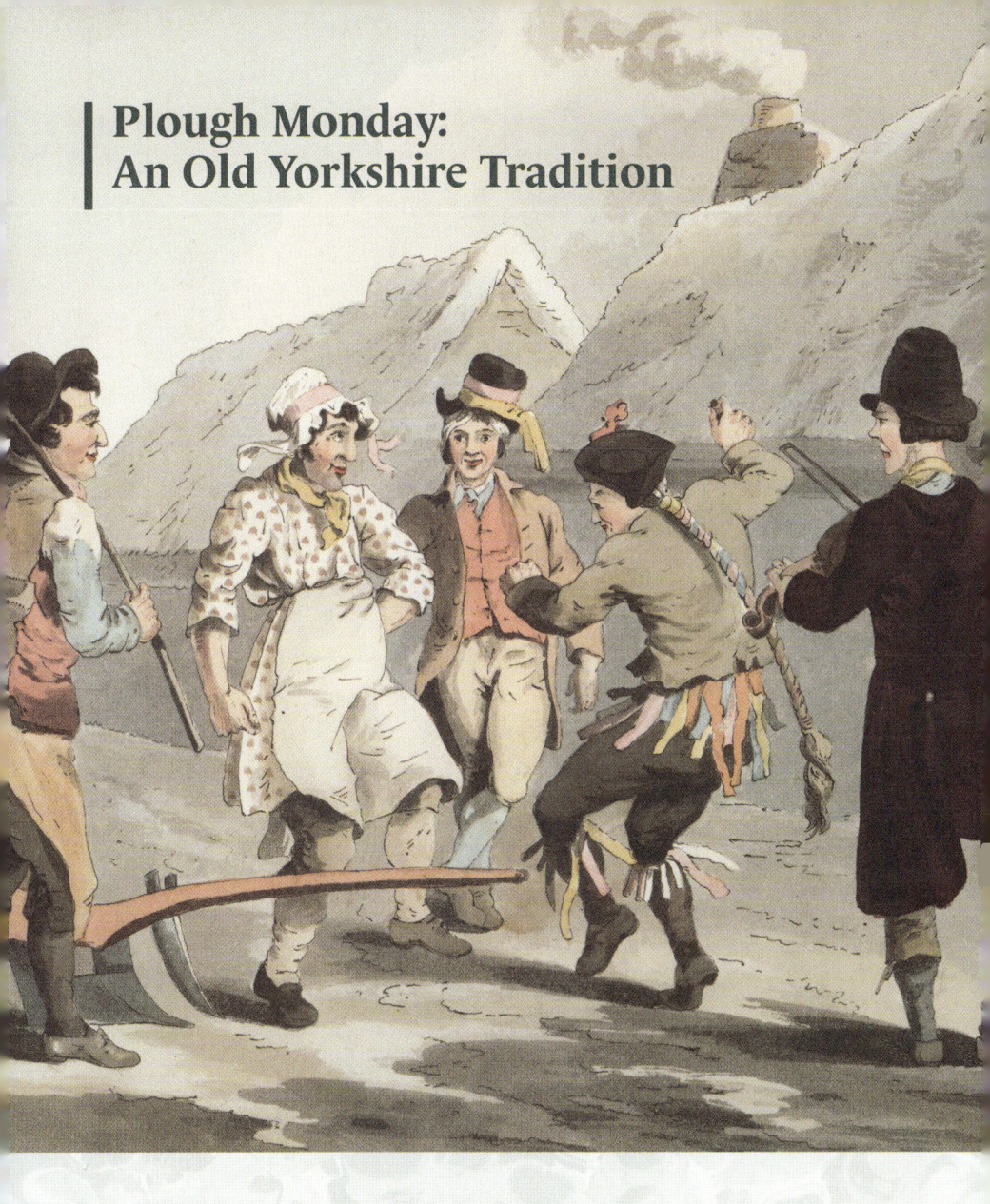

✦ Plough Monday, or the first Monday in January after Twelfth Night, is traditionally the end of the ploughman's holiday. An old Yorkshire custom to 'bless the plough' involved young farming lads dragging a plough through the streets to the church to be blessed at the start of the agricultural year. The pageant included a comical procession of costumed characters bringing to mind the Mummers or Morris-dancers at Christmas.

Cloggers in Arncliffe

Mr T. Watson's photograph captures a rare glimpse into a peaceful but bygone industry – the cutting and preparation of wood for clog-making. It was taken in 1913, deep in Arncliffe Woods near the Esk Valley village of Glaisdale.

A local resident, Mr A.S. Frank, confirmed that the picture was of the Moore family – father and two sons. The widow of one of the sons lived at Egton Bridge and descendants of the old man lived at Grosmont. For many years the cloggers worked in Egton, Glaisdale and Goathland districts and it was on several occasions that Mr Frank remembered their encampment in the Beckhole and Arncliffe woods.

Sycamore and alder were used for making clogs – beech was regarded as too heavy. This was one of the very few uses to which the sycamore's soft wood was suitable. As the photograph reveals, comparatively young trees were used.

A note from an Egton diary in 1852 mentions that 'On March 16th, the cloggers came'. In other words it was the beginning of the cutting season, which usually lasted until October.

Wood was sawn into lengths, the lengths were split and the clog soles then roughly shaped by hand. A specially designed machine imparted a high degree of finish to the soles before they were stacked. Most of the soles were loaded into waggons and dispatched to various Lancashire towns, where the later stages of clog manufacture were carried on. Mrs Moore, however, stated that the old Mr Moore was able to fit the leather uppers and irons himself, and that he did actually turn out the finished clog – no doubt this was his winter work, catering for local demand.

At the time of the photograph, clogs were used universally by workers in the West Riding woollen mills and in the cotton mills of Lancashire. Here they insulated the mill workers from the cold, stone-flagged floors, which later were to prove so hard on fancy footwear.

Clogs were also in general use for farm work and were commonly seen hanging in the Whitby boot shops. In winter time one often saw school children and labourers wearing them. Warm and dry in snow and wet, they cost less than half the price of a pair of boots.

The 1914–18 war brought the industry to an end. Increased wartime earnings ushered in silk stockings and fancy footwear for the previously clog-shod mill girls. Men, too, discarded clogs and the demand for them almost ceased. Mr R.L. Foster recalled that the last camp of the cloggers on Egton Estate was in 1916; it was in the Warren, across the river opposite the Manor.

Based on a Whitby Naturalists' Club Report from 22 September 1945

Clog Dancing

✦ English clog-dancing is a percussive form of dance producing rhythmic beats through intricate footwork. It grew in popularity in the early days of the Industrial Revolution and spanned the whole of the Victorian era.

In Northern England, a particular style of clog dancing developed in the cotton mills of Lancashire from around 1820. Here, men, women and children wore wooden-soled clogs to work and typically spent their waking hours at spinning machines or powered looms. Tapping their feet to the sounds and rhythms of the machinery, they developed dances to suit their loose-fitting work clothes and weighty clogs. Copying each other and inventing new steps, the mill workers challenged themselves in competitions during work breaks. Many also danced at home, in pubs and in the street.

Music-hall performers took up clog dancing in tighter-fitting and lighter clogs, taking the dances to greater levels of complexity.

A Roberts loom in a weaving shed in 1835.

Lancashire mill girls in 1874 relaxing at lunchtime – detail showing English style clogs worn by some of the girls.

Clog dancing declined after the First World War but a revival from the late 1950s was led by dancers including Pat Tracey, Sam Sherry and Alex Woodcock. Today there are clog-dancing teams dotted around the UK, including one in Glaisdale on the North York Moors – a fitting location given the tradition of clog-making in the area.

Performances of clog dancing and other forms of step- or percussive dance, such as morris dancing, can be seen at folk festivals around North Yorkshire, including Saltburn and Whitby. Clog dancing evolved into tap dancing in America, combining West African and British dance traditions.

A Yacre of Land – a Folk Song

My father he left me a yacre[1] of land
Yacre of land, yacre of land,
My father he left me a yacre of land,
On Christmas Day in the morning.

I ploughed it with an old stack[2] plod
An old stack plod, an old stack plod,
I ploughed it with an old stack plod,
On Christmas Day in the morning.

I harrowed it with a bunch of briars,
A bunch of briars, a bunch of briars,
I harrowed it with a bunch of briars,
On Christmas day in the morning.

I sowed it with a peppercorn,
A peppercorn, a peppercorn,
I sowed it with a peppercorn,
On Christmas Day in the morning.

I reaped it with an old tup's horn,
An old tup's horn, an old tup's horn,
I reaped it with an old tup's horn,
On Christmas day in the morning.

I laid it on a bumble bee's back,
A bumble bee's back, a bumble bee's back
I laid it on a bumble bee's back,
On Christmas Day in the morning.

I threshed it with a wimble[3] straw,
A wimble straw, a wimble straw,
I threshed it with a wimble straw,
On Christmas Day in the morning.

I flayed it with a butterfly's wing,
A butterfly's wing, a butterfly's wing,
I flayed it with a butterfly's wing,
On Christmas Day in the morning.

I sold it all for one pound ten,
One pound ten, one pound ten,
I sold it all for one pound ten,
On Christmas Day in the morning.

'A Yacre of Land' has a similar tune to the ancient Christmas Carol 'I Saw Three Ships Come Sailing In'.

1   'Yacre' – an acre
2   'Stack plod' – probably a corruption of stack (or stock) plough
3   'Wimble' – an instrument for boring into soft ground

Ralph Vaughan Williams' Visit to Westerdale

Ralph Vaughan Williams
Ralph Vaughan Williams was born in 1872 in Down Ampney, Gloucestershire. From a well-to-do family he went on to become one of Britain's greatest classical composers, although he struggled as a young musician and composer to find his true voice. It was his discovery of the indigenous music of his native country – traditional folk song – that showed him the way forward and inspired his future musical output.

At the turn of the twentieth century, a great upsurge of interest in traditional folk music of Britain led many musicians to begin collecting songs and music that until then had never been written down. Vaughan Williams became an avid collector, travelling around the counties collecting hundreds of traditional songs and melodies that may have been lost had he not done so.

On 13 July 1904, Vaughan Williams, aged 32, was in North Yorkshire when he paid a visit to the Duncombe Arms in Westerdale (now a private house). Here a Mr Greenwood sang a song called 'A Yacre of Land' and this simple ditty with its wry words was captured in musical notation by Vaughan Williams for posterity. With no convenient electronic recording apparatus in those days, he had to write down what he heard, transcribing the melody into musical notation and noting down the lyrics – a skilful procedure as the country singers sometimes faulted on the words, sang off-key and gave numerous variations of the tune.

The lyrics for 'A Yacre of Land' are simple and humorous. It is in the same mode as the well-known folk song, 'Scarborough Fair' in which impossible

Folk music tradition carries on: Tony O'Donnell at The Duke of Wellington, Danby.

tasks are set for an ardent would-be suitor.

Another song collected on the same night was 'Young William', also known as 'Kiss me in the Dark', sung by Willy Knaggs, a labourer and church sexton who played the 'bass fiddle'. Knaggs clearly didn't find the rather suggestive tale was inappropriate for his office. Vaughan Williams decided on 6/8 time but notes 'this may have been common time (4/4)'. His handwritten notes and lyrics can be viewed via a link to the online Vaughan Williams Memorial Library: https://www.vwml.org/record/RVW2/3/4

The trip to North Yorkshire nearly cost Vaughan Williams his life. While bathing off a deserted and rocky beach at Robin Hood's Bay, he very nearly drowned. The sea was rougher than he thought and he could not scramble back onto the rocks. He had almost decided to give up and let himself drown when a wave washed him on to the shore.[1]

AINSLEY

---

1   *R.V.W. A Biography of Ralph Vaughan Williams*, Ursula Vaughan Williams, 1993

The Krampus Run Has Come to Whitby

A tradition in parts of Europe on 5 December, the Eve of the Feast of Saint Nicholas, is for Saint Nicholas to visit homes and give gifts to good children. He is accompanied by his dark counterpart, 'The Krampus', who teases and punishes naughty boys and girls. This horned figure, half-goat, half-demon, can be found in folklore across Europe and is typically celebrated in festivals in Austria, Bavaria, Croatia, Czech Republic, Hungary, Northern Italy including South Tyrol, Slovakia and Slovenia.

The festival, or parade, known as 'The Krampus Run' was held in the UK for the first time in 2015 when it came to Whitby, brought by arts-based group, Decadent Drawing CIC.[1] The Whitby event was born out of an art session held at La Rosa Hotel[2] and has its own special stamp. A good introduction to how the Krampus Run came to Whitby can be found via the Decadent Drawing website.[3]

Since the first event in 2015 the Whitby Krampus Run has grown into a popular annual celebration. The stills shown here are from a video recording

Still from video © Rith Rathor

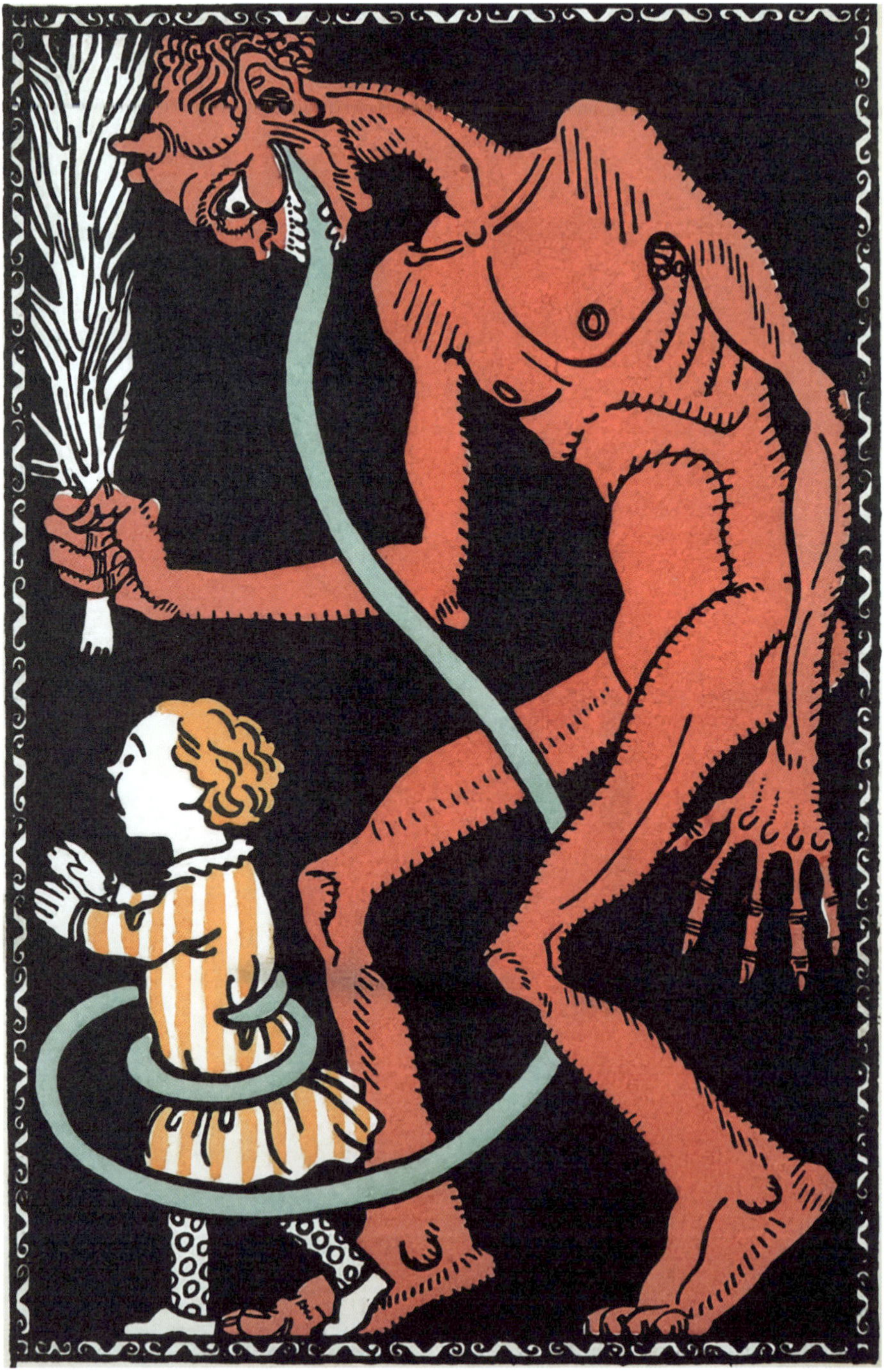

Stills from video © Rith Rathor

of the December 2022 parade made by Ruth Rathor. Her full video can be viewed on YouTube at: https://youtu.be/Skm3ZPP2mnw

Whitby's newly introduced event originating from European folklore is weaving yet more colour into the vibrant local culture. It livens up the town in the run-up to Christmas and adds to the spectacular pageants already provided by the Goth festivals and Bram Stoker International Film Festival.

| Opposite: 'Krampus with a child', postcard from around 1911.

---

1   www.decadentdrawing.com
2   www.larosa.co.uk
3   Or go directly to: https://express.adobe.com/page/SabqDn8I1AN4L

© Andrew Marsay